Lighthouse Chronicles

TWENTY YEARS
on the
B.C. LIGHTS

Flo Anderson

HARBOUR PUBLISHING

Published by
HARBOUR PUBLISHING
P.O. Box 219
Madeira Park, BC Canada V0N 2H0

Cover design and page composition by Martin Nichols, Lionheart Graphics.

All photographs by Flo Anderson and her family, unless credited otherwise.

Front cover photograph of the Race Rocks lighthouse by Chris Jaksa.

We acknowledge the financial support of the Government of Canada through the Book Publishing Industry Development Program and the Province of British Columbia through the British Columbia Arts Council for our publishing activities.

Canadian Cataloguing in Publication Data

Anderson, Flo, 1924–
    Lighthouse chronicles

    Includes index.
    ISBN 1-55017-181-X

    1. Anderson, Flo, 1924– 2. Lighthouse keepers—British Columbia—Biography. I. Title.
VK1027.B7A52 1998   387.1'55'092   C98-910225-4

THE CANADA COUNCIL | LE CONSEIL DES ARTS
FOR THE ARTS | DU CANADA
SINCE 1957 | DEPUIS 1957

This book is dedicated to my family:
Trev, my partner, researcher, critic;
Stan, who introduced me to the world of computers and
provided expertise, instruction and encouragement;
Janet, for proofreading;
Beth, for photographs, art input
and for being my personal editor;
Adrienne, for her loving support;
Jeff, for computer upgrading and advice;
and Garry, for adding to the family story
with his unique experiences.

CONTENTS

Lennard Island

December 9, 1961–June 15, 1963

The crew drew up the gangplank and hauled in the mooring lines as we stepped aboard ship in Victoria. The Coast Guard vessel gently moved forward, and I saw ahead the Johnson Street bridge lift in readiness for our passage. A new adventure began as we glided under the bridge and headed out to sea, past the beautiful inner harbour of Victoria with the ivy-covered Empress Hotel, lush emerald lawns and distinguished legislative buildings. There at the bridge, unexpectedly, was Dad, waving and calling "Bon Voyage!" A lump came to my throat. Only minutes before, we had said our goodbyes at their home before the taxi sped us away to the dock.

In this quiet moment, I finally had time to think back over the last frantic weeks since the Department of Transport had notified Trev he had qualified as a lightkeeper. Trev had accepted immediately. He had been at loose ends since his release from the air force after twenty years. His many years training and working as a radio operator and later as radar fighter controller were not recognized as experience in civilian life, although he had flown all over the world and basically done the same work as an aircraft controller at civilian airports. So, on the suggestion of a friend who knew of Trev's penchant for the outdoors and the secluded life, Trev applied for a lightkeeper position. For some time, we heard nothing. Meanwhile, his employer in Victoria transferred him to Vancouver, where his job as troubleshooter required him to drive daily through desperate traffic to far-ranging parts of the city. Confusion and city horn-honkers drove him to distraction, while he dreamed of the wide open spaces of the wilderness. Just as we settled into our new home in Vancouver, suitably sized and located, rented with an option to buy, we got notification of Trev's acceptance as a lightkeeper. What to do? (What a decision!)

Lightstations were a mystery to us. We knew very little about them other than a weekend visit we had made to Discovery Island near Victoria. The lightkeeper there had been the perfect host and the island was entrancing—but we were visiting, not actually residing on a secluded island. The thought of living on a lightstation with its uniqueness was intriguing and yet frightening when we considered the isolation, the responsibility for home schooling, and the unknown. But I knew it would be better for the family to have Trev more content, and I could handle a challenge.

We had selected Lennard Island from a list of ten available positions because it was very important to me that a rescue lifeboat was close by (three miles away) and came regularly to the lightstation from Tofino. Over the years when Trev's work had taken him away, I had had to handle all emergencies with the four children—Garry, now sixteen, Stan, fourteen, Beth, twelve and Adrienne, four.

Also, I was familiar with Lennard Island and Tofino—names that had woven through my earlier years in various ways. I remembered hearing stories from my father, who had taught school in Tofino before the First World War, arriving there February 22, 1911 on his twenty-second birthday. As a child I had heard how he rowed three miles on open ocean in a small rowboat to Lennard Island—a daring feat, especially for a novice like him. As well, he had boarded with the family of the former lightkeeper, Mr. Garrad, in Tofino. Some of the Garrad children attended Dad's school. Dad then bought property at the edge of Tofino Village, built himself a house and became even more connected to the community. He stayed until the war broke out, then left to join the army.

Many years later, Mr. Garrad, the courtly old gentleman, came to Victoria with his youngest daughter and her husband. I visited them often and heard more stories of Tofino. He also impressed my sister and me, too young to date, by inviting us to shows and treating us as such ladies.

Trev had also had some experience with Lennard Island. When he returned from overseas in 1943, he was sent to Tofino Airport. As a courtesy to my father, he visited some old-timers in Tofino who just happened to be going to Lennard Island that day and took him along for a visit. How strange for us, soon after our arrival in December of 1961, to find an old log book with the record of his visit eighteen years earlier.

I too had visited Tofino, once with my father and sisters on the ship *Uchuck* (we called it *Upchuck*) from Port Alberni, and again via the road which finally opened in 1961. Our car was one of the first to drive the road. My father had said that a road to Port Alberni would take fifty years to build, as only one mile from Tofino through his property had been built before he left to join the army in 1914. It was a great event for him to travel the road, rough as it was, fifty years later.

The instructions from the District Manager, our boss in Victoria, were extensive. Crating all our furniture was our first priority since, we were informed, it would be transported by ship, offloaded into a workboat and hauled by bonnet sling on a carriage up a cable to the island. Whatever *that* meant! We realized we would have to reduce our four-bedroom household effects considerably. Not only were we restricted to what we could take but we had to pay the moving charges from Vancouver to Victoria, and we had just paid for the move from Courtenay to Vancouver. Trev went to a moving company to get instructions to crate our own furniture. We weeded out our belongings down to the barest minimum—foolishly, in our great haste and ignorance. We did not think ahead to a time when we would come off the lightstation occasionally for holidays, business or medical care, so we gave away the children's ski equipment, bicycles, etc., and sold our two cars for almost nothing. Most heartbreaking of all, we sold our piano, which we had recently painstakingly refinished to match our maple furniture. It would have been wiser to transport the piano to Victoria and leave it with my parents. Hindsight is so clear!

An important part of our planning and preparing was the education of our four children. We had talked it over with them and explained that they would be doing correspondence courses under our supervision. The BC government had developed and produced courses for each year from kindergarten through eight years of elementary grades and four years of high school. We registered all the children and even arranged a kindergarten course for the youngest, who might otherwise be a disturbing influence while the others were studying. These were comprehensive courses, and we had to order all the books for four different grades plus lesson plans and papers for several months. At times, the responsibility of educating four children seemed overwhelming.

Next in importance was the matter of supplies. We could hardly imagine how to estimate the kinds and amounts of provisions required for a month or six weeks. I concentrated on calculating for staples—a hundred pounds of flour, twenty-five pounds of sugar, a case of margarine, a large bag of instant dried milk, cases of different canned vegetables and meats, and then carefully selected fresh produce and meat. We did not know what kind of storage facilities were available on the lightstation so included only a few days' worth of perishables. The fact that the Tofino lifeboat made a weekly trip to Lennard Island, weather permitting, gave us a sense that we had some backup. (Little did we know that "the weather permitting" didn't permit much during the winter!) We also had to arrange for a grocer who would package the groceries to withstand the extraordinary handling involved, and who would extend credit since our future orders would have to be sent a month in advance of the groceries being taken to the tender (the ship that services lightstations).

After the arrangements were made, there was more time to imagine the trip itself. Near the end of our hectic preparations to move, I lay awake one night remembering one line in the letter from the Department of Transport, about being taken from ship to shore by workboat. Suddenly I was struck with a frightening image. Knowing practically nothing of ships, all I could picture were scenes from movies where a ship's emergency had occurred, a rope ladder had been thrown over the side and people had to scramble down this precarious support as it swung with the heaving sea. I could visualize myself trying

The Coast Guard vessel Camsell *carried us to our new home at Lennard Island in December 1961. We made several stops along the way, as the ship was the supply tender that carried mail and supplies to lightstations along the west coast of Vancouver Island.*

to hand Adrienne to someone in the workboat as it dipped out of reach with a swell. I sat up in bed and said quite firmly that I simply could not go, I could *not* go. Trev tiredly turned over and said, "What's wrong now?" I explained my imaginings and he informed me just as firmly that ships had things called accommodation ladders, which meant that one just walked down a ramp into the boat below. He even took me to the outer wharf in Victoria to show me the ladders in use with the freighters at dock there.

Still, the fear of the rope ladder stayed with me, even as we enjoyed our days aboard the ship on the way to Lennard Island. The weather was sunny and beautiful and the sea fairly calm. Even when we reached the long rolling swells of the open Pacific Ocean, and some queasy feelings eventually led to intermittent seasickness, the voyage was fascinating. The crew was so very obliging, showing us all over the ship. The boys were particularly intrigued with the engine room, and the captain then showed them the mysteries of the bridge. Delightful meals were served on white linen tablecloths. We had marvellous informative conversations at the captain's table. I found out later that it is not often a family with four children attempts a life on a lightstation, so I guess we were a curiosity to the crew.

We were aboard the *Camsell*, an icebreaker that was used in the Arctic in the summer and as a tender servicing lightstations in the winter. To quote from an early letter of Stan's:

> On the *Camsell* there are seven engines, three generators, and four power units. The propellers are eleven feet nine inches in diameter and the shafts are seventeen inches in diameter when they leave the hull of the ship. The ship is two hundred and twenty-four feet long, forty-eight feet across and sixteen foot draft. There is a small hanger aft for a Bell helicopter. Garry and I have our own cabin. It has a washbasin, bench, closet, double dresser and bunk beds.

For five days after we had reached the open ocean, the ship worked slowly up the west coast of Vancouver Island, a lonely, heavily forested area with deep undergrowth that looked to us to be inhabited only by lightstation personnel and a few rustic hermits. The supply tender serviced the lights on a regular monthly trip, and we were aboard the Christmas run with special supplies for the lightkeepers and their families—choice delicacies like *fresh* milk, *fresh* vegetables—plus parcels and extra letters.

The ship's first call after Race Rocks was Carmanah, high on a steep cliff. The new keeper was transported from the ship by helicopter. We then had our first view of supplies being transferred from the hold of the ship to a bonnet sling to the workboat bobbing at the side of the ship, and thence to the shore where a long steel cable stretched from the high cliff over water to a rock offshore. A carriage sizzled down the cable to a release mechanism that dropped the hook on the cable to the workboat. There the crew attached the bonnet sling filled with furniture or other goods. The winch was started and the loaded sling dangled its way to a platform at the high elevation.

We soon learned that when weather and sea conditions were fair, the offloading went smoothly. However, if adverse conditions prevailed, timing became all-important. When the swells were large, the workboat could be moving up and down as much as fifteen feet. It was

The village of Tofino, which was very small in December 1961, was our only lifeline from Lennard Island besides the supply tender. It was the closest town, and most important, a rescue lifeboat was located there.

then critical to attach the bonnet sling to the hook when the boat was on the crest of its upward motion so that as the boat went down, the sling was lifted clear of the boat. If the timing was off, the rising water could overtake the sling—dousing the contents, sometimes even dumping them into the sea, lost forever. The workboat made as many trips as necessary to offload groceries, mail, hardware, furniture, trunks and other supplies.

Another fifteen miles along the coast, again high on a cliff, perched Pachena Point lighthouse. This too was a wild stretch of coast. We could well imagine the plight of any shipwrecked person, even if lucky enough to reach this forbidding shoreline, trying to scramble ashore on treacherous rocks and being thrown about by the ocean swell. The next station, Cape Beale, stands at the entrance to Barkley Sound but was hidden from our view on board ship, as we had anchored on the other side of the headland from the light in the lee of a projection of land. We could see the workboat disappear around the point on its trips ashore. The ship then headed for Ucluelet, a small fishing village on the north side of the entrance to Barkley Sound, where we docked for a few hours. The children had a chance to stretch their legs and explore the village. That night the ship

Most of my information about getting on and off a ship had come from the movies, where people clung precariously to dangling rope ladders. My husband Trevor assured me that we would board the workboat by walking down a ramp, but on the way to Lennard, whenever the Camsell stopped to service a lightstation, a workboat was lowered to the water and a rope ladder was thrown over the side of the ship.

anchored in the protected sound where we could see the twinkling lights of both Bamfield and Ucluelet reflected on the still waters.

Next day we watched with mounting anticipation as the ship weighed anchor and, hardly disturbing the motionless water, slipped into the open Pacific. We passed Amphitrite Point at the northern entrance to Barkley Sound and beautiful Long Beach, where waves gently lapped the miles of glistening sand. A few hours later we excitedly caught our first glimpse of Lennard Island, our new home, silhouetted against a glorious sunset. The island appeared quite small, but large enough to have some tall evergreens. This landfall light, established in 1904 midway along the west coast of Vancouver Island, was the first land light a ship's crew saw after crossing the Pacific Ocean. Thus it was rated as a first class light. It was too late in the day to offload our belongings. We watched the light winking as we glided past into Tofino and tied up at the government wharf.

Tofino was a typical fishing village with a couple of tall wood-frame stores on the wharf built on piles over water. The village proper perched on the hill above, overlooking Browning Passage and Opitsaht Indian Village on the opposite shore. The Maquinna Hotel dominated the scene. It had been built just after the war, using materials from the wartime air force buildings at Tofino Airport. This was indeed opportune since building supplies, especially nails and lumber, were scarce during and after the war. The population at that time, December 1961, was about five hundred. We were too excited at the prospect of what the morrow would bring to pay much attention to the village that night although it would be our nearest civilization.

The next day finally arrived and within a short time we were anchored near Lennard Island. Over went the workboat onto the water. Trev and the boys scrambled down the rope ladder into the boat and were off on the bounding main to help unload our belongings as they arrived on shore. The girls and I were told to wait until the job was completed. It took a long time. We ate lunch as the two workboats passed each other, ferrying our furniture to its new home.

Lunch over, we stationed ourselves on deck once again, I with mounting anxiety for the fateful call to clamber down that rope ladder. Suddenly a voice said, "Oh, there you are, Mrs. Anderson." It was the captain. "I was wondering if you would prefer to go ashore in the helicopter?"

It was all I could do to maintain my dignity and not fling my arms around his neck, saying, "Yes, yes, yes!"

In very short order we were strapped into the helicopter, and minutes later we landed on a flat, long, grassy area between two glistening white beaches. The boys were there, open-mouthed, to greet us. The pilot asked them if they would like to go for a ride, and two thrilled teenaged boys got a wonderful aerial view of their new domain.

To get to our new home, we followed a path to an opening in the salal bushes at the edge of the clearing where the helicopter had landed. Eventually we came to three white frame houses snugged together in a hollow. The shell path led us past a small, fairly new house and I thought, "This house is quite modern with good possibilities." We crunched farther along the path to the far side of the big, old, rundown centre dwelling which was at a much higher elevation than the two smaller, newer houses. No one was around. It felt eerie, as if unseen eyes were watching us.

We climbed a flight of stairs at the side of the dwelling to a tres-tled walk that led west to a long white garagelike engine house and east to the boathouse and supply landing area. Two-by-fours had been nailed to the walk, forming rails so that a cart carrying heavy supplies could be pushed along it more easily. At right angles to this walkway was a ramp leading to the light tower, high on the point and directly in front of the centre house. At the juncture of these two walks was an uninviting heavy white door with a smallish glass panel near the top. We eagerly opened the door and walked into our new home.

My heart sank as I looked around the very old dwelling. I had been prepared for the isolation, the responsibility of the children's education, the grocery challenge, etc., but never in my wildest imag-inings did I think we would have to step back into the nineteenth century and become pioneers, especially with a federal government position. The huge kitchen had bare wooden floors and a wood and coal stove, its door propped shut with a stick. Off to one side was the bathroom with an old white claw-footed bathtub, hand basin and toilet. On the wall was a pump with a big wooden handle with which we would have to pump water to the tank in the attic which then fed the the faucets and toilet by gravity. Rainwater was collected from the roof through downspouts to a concrete cistern about the size of a garage located outside.

A door on another wall of the kitchen opened into a long pantry with cupboards and working counter on one side, and on the other side, a counter and sink under a window overlooked one of the other two houses. There was no fridge and we had not brought one with us. Instead, at the far end of the pantry was a cooler with slatted shelves and mesh-covered openings through the outside wall.

Another door in the kitchen led into the living room and off this room were two smallish bedrooms. Stan said, "Man, what closets!" A massive brick fireplace dominated the sitting room. The chimney had a straight flue which, we later found, drafted any heat straight up to the open skies. The floor was rough bare wood. There was no furnace

Unloading all our supplies, furniture and household effects at Lennard Island was a lengthy procedure. The Camsell anchored near Lennard Island and two small workboats went back and forth, ferrying our belongings to the island with the help of a winch, cable and bonnet sling.

19

in the cellar—a high, open crawl space whose only use seemed to be a place for the wind to whistle up through the cracks in the floor. We realized that the only heat for this dreary old place would come from the broken-down kitchen stove and the cavernous fireplace.

There was no welcome wagon for us, and no one paid a visit, although we could see that the other two houses were occupied and we knew the senior keeper and the other junior keeper lived at Lennard too. Eventually Trev met with the other two men to arrange shifts. Each man was required to stand watch for eight hours—the senior keeper took the daylight hours and the two juniors alternated the evening and midnight shifts. The men were also expected to help if necessary when not on shift. I was too busy settling our household and getting the schoolwork organized to even get outside for a couple of weeks. I finally met the other junior keeper's wife and her little girl, but did not see the senior keeper's wife for some time.

We set up and made the beds, and dug out some dishes and food to prepare a meal. Trev went to find some wood to light the stove, but after searching all corners found none in the cellar. He rounded up the boys and they gathered small bits of wet driftwood from the beach. Dinner was delayed a long time! Trev had not brought his chain saw or other tools, assuming this type of equipment would be available on a lightstation. It was a dismal beginning.

But the next morning we took a second look and saw some possibilities. We set to work. Over the next few days we painted the wooden floors, arranged the furniture, put rugs down and drapes up, and gradually the barn became a home. We put the boys into one of the bedrooms, made a bed settee for Beth in the corner by the fireplace and set up a small cot in one corner of our room for Adrienne.

As the days went by, the problem of keeping warm was always with us. I ripped out old sweaters and knitted wool socks as fast as I could. The boys helped Trev cut driftwood with a hand saw, but the wood was still dripping wet.

The primitive heating facilities became more understandable when we found out that the station had been electrified only two months previously. A couple of weeks after we arrived, the electric light in the tower, which had been converted from a kerosene mantle-type light to a mickey-mouse setup with one electric bulb, was turned on for the first time. But even though we officially had electricity, the generators were off eight hours a day—usually during the same hours I would be cooking, washing, vacuuming, etc. This was a major handicap when trying to arrange all the new duties into a timetable.

We organized the school-day by putting Stan near the front door, Beth in a corner of the living room and Garry in a bedroom. Adrienne stayed in the kitchen with me, and we installed a big blackboard at her level so she could run in and put her ideas in chalk. I made a regular tour to answer questions and give directions to reference material. When they could not solve a problem, I would sit down and help them work through the difficulty. They became very good at searching through reference material for their own information. They also became very adept at finding ways to entertain themselves when they were supposed to be doing schoolwork.

The boys were extremely interested in the winch, carriage and cable arrangement used to bring supplies ashore. They bugged their dad to help them get accurate measurements, and gradually they built a working model. It was powered by a gasoline motor they scrounged from their dad, who had used it when building airplane models. They set up this working model between their two desks, one in the living room and one in the bedroom. We greatly admired their ingenuity until I realized they were spending more time writing and sending notes back and forth than studying!

Our one rule was that after the day's schoolwork was completed, the rest of the day was ours. Often the whole family set out to explore. On our first expedition, we walked through a hole in the protective wall of salal, the stalks as big as small trees, that surrounded the houses. On the other side was the clearing for the helicopter pad with two dazzling white beaches, one on either side of the pad. As we went strolling along the beaches, we noticed that the sand was really made up of small shells, endless in variety. The most fascinating was a pure white cone-shaped shell called a wentletrap. We later read that this shell had been used as money in certain parts of the world. We noticed acorn and goose-necked barnacles, limpets, whelks and mussels on the rocks. In the water were various-coloured sea urchins and anemones,

Watching the abundant sea life in the tide pools on Lennard Island was one of the children's favourite activities—except for the time Stan raced home to report that something really weird had grabbed his leg. Adrienne went out later to investigate more closely.

purple, red brittle and orange sun starfish, chitons, crabs, nudibranchs, sea cucumbers, squid and jellyfish—a veritable cornucopia of colour.

The Pacific Ocean continuously washed the shores of our new home and provided us with an endless source of marine animal discoveries. One of the kids' great pleasures was to search the tidepools for the many forms of sea life found there when the tide was low. One particular pool was waist deep and fascinating to explore, as it had many small caves and boulders in it where hidden creatures lurked. One day Stan was busy searching for whatever might be in the pool, when to our surprise and dismay he let out a bloodcurdling yell, leaped straight up and almost ran across the top of the water in his haste to exit the pool. After he had calmed down, he told us something really weird had grabbed his leg. We soon found a seven-foot octopus nestled under a large rock. It had reached out with one of its tentacles to examine Stan's leg!

There were starfish of every type, from large twenty-legged sun starfish to tiny brittle starfish. On one of their excursions, unbeknownst to their father and me, the boys and Beth decided to see how many starfish they could find in one day. They collected them at low tide and stacked them atop a high, secluded rock. When I called them home, they simply forgot about their project. Some days later a most peculiar pungent odour began wafting across the island, and it didn't dissipate until a gale cleared the rock of decaying starfish.

Sometimes we even found small intact glass balls washed up by the sea. We knew that the large ones, used as floats for Japanese fishnets, drifted onto the sand beaches of the west coast, but at Lennard Island any that came ashore were hurled up by the mighty swells and destroyed on the rocky terrain. One day Trev found fragments of what looked like a large one. He gathered all the pieces and on many an ensuing midnight shift he tried to fit together this spherical jigsaw puzzle. I came out in the mornings to see it taking shape on the table with a note inside and in large print, reading DO NOT TOUCH. Weeks later he had all the pieces together except one about the size of a playing card. Trev returned to the rocks where he had found all the other bits, dug around and lifted stones, and found another section. He tried it and it fit perfectly. He had completed the sphere! We now had our one large glass ball, but with a note inside. It was quite a conversation piece.

To further explore the island, we realized, we would have to cut into the dank, dense undergrowth. Trev decided to start whacking out a path around the island, not only for our own enjoyment, but for anyone who might come ashore on other parts of the island and need to find their way to the houses. Even though the island wasn't that big—about eighteen acres—the profuse bush was impassable. While Trev wielded the machete, I trailed behind thrusting the slashing to one side. It was slow going.

In the meantime, the teenagers cleared their own area in the centre of the island. Then they tied a sturdy rope in a tree and had great sport swinging out and letting go of the rope to drop onto the salal, which was so dense it acted as a spring mattress.

Gradually we got to know the buildings on the island, and the workings of the light. The tower of this landfall light was a wooden structure, four storeys high. Inside it looked as if it had been designed to accommodate living quarters but had never been used as such. From the ground floor to the next level was a twenty-foot flight of stairs. The next two floors, equal distance apart, were joined by a series of ladders, which finally reached the lantern room.

This glass-enclosed area contained the light itself, a mantle-type light similar to a Coleman gasoline lantern, but considerably larger. The mantle was about three inches in diameter and ten inches tall. Around the wall of the lamp room were numerous ports that could be adjusted to control ventilation. These ports were very important items because if the ventilation was not correct, the lamp would begin to smoke, the soot would get on the prism lenses, and the brilliance of the light would be reduced. The job of polishing the lenses was not only tedious but unpleasant. They had to be rubbed down with methylated spirits, then polished with a chamois or flannel cloth. On a warm day the fumes from the alcohol could be quite nauseating, especially combined with the effect of the prisms, which distorted our vision.

To light the mantle, we started by filling a five-gallon tank with kerosene. Then, with a pump similar to an old tire pump, another air tank of equal size was pumped up until the pressure was 40 pounds per

The lantern room of the Lennard Island lightstation was a glass-enclosed area at the top of a four-storey tower, and a series of clockwork gears rotated the four huge prism lenses—each one eight feet in diameter. It could be quite disorienting to stand among them!

square inch (psi), as indicated by a gauge on the tank. Below the heat tubes extending from the ten-inch mantle was a trough into which alcohol was poured, then lit. When the flame was hot enough (judged by trial and error) the valves to the air and kerosene tanks were opened so that the light would fire up properly. Trev was relieved he only had to deal with this procedure for a couple of weeks before it was changed to an electric bulb.

Clockwork machinery rotated the platform that held the set of four huge (eight-foot) prism lenses. They floated on a massive round container filled with a ton of mercury. The system had to be checked regularly as the level of mercury could alter with changes in temperature. At that time there were no health rules requiring masks, so on a hot summer day a keeper working in the lamp room no doubt breathed considerable mercury vapour. If you stood in the middle of the four lenses you would just about go wacky, because the prisms distorted your vision and appeared to be rotating in the opposite direction.

The system of clockwork gears, much like that in a grandfather clock, was controlled by a governor and powered by a six-hundred-pound weight suspended on a wire cable from a drum. When a brake was released, the weight gradually descended all the way to the ground floor of the tower, about sixty feet, and then had to be rewound onto the drum. This drum had a series of gears that would allow the weight to exert energy to the table as it was being wound up. The handle had to be wound four hundred and twenty-three times every two hours, which took about twenty minutes. For this procedure Trev switched hands regularly, and he developed strong shoulder muscles on both sides.

The whole mechanism needed a lot of maintenance and the light had to be watched constantly. Any change in wind direction or velocity meant Trev had to climb to the top to adjust the ventilators. In stormy weather and high winds the tower moved enough so that sometimes the drive weight jammed in the chute and the light stopped rotating. This required another climb up the ladders to correct the problem.

The engine house was another building of significance. It was a white, red-roofed, warehouselike building which contained a fuel tank, lube oil barrels, fog engines, foghorn compressors and tanks of compressed air to activate the foghorn. Like the beacon light, each piece of mechanical apparatus required constant maintenance and repair. The fuel tank had to be laboriously refilled with diesel fuel hand pumped from forty-five-gallon drums. Once a year approximately two hundred of these drums were offloaded from the tender via a workboat, four at a time, and manhandled, rolled and sometimes trollied from the winch house loading platform along the entire length of the elevated ramp to the engine house. They were stored side by side and one on top of the other at the side of the engine building.

The foghorn engines, two Fairbanks 9-horsepower single-cylinder engines, were connected to two compressors twelve feet away by two circular twenty-foot leather belts. Because the belts were very susceptible to breaking, a number of spare belts were kept on hand. This way the beltless engine could be stopped and another engine started to avoid any interruption of the foghorn during fog. The broken belt was repaired later. To be started, the fog engine was hand cranked, and it could be very temperamental—not easily handled by irascible people.

One time, after the senior keeper had been on duty on an intensely foggy day, Trev found parts of a broken handle strewn across the engine room, obviously broken in a fit of rage.

From the drive pulley on the engine there was another series of belts and pulleys that operated the code device (on the back wall), which determined that station's unique foghorn signal. This coder had a notched four-inch brass disk. When a mechanical arm dropped into the notch, a small valve was depressed that allowed compressed air from the tanks to flow to the horn and create a noisy blast of air. Other valves and diaphragms determined the length and frequency of the blasts. It seemed to me the engine room was a tangled mass of belts and pulleys, but it all worked well.

The foghorn at Lennard Island was a Type F horn, operating on a sound frequency of nearly two hundred cycles per second, and could be heard fifteen miles away. You could feel the horn as well as hear it and see its effect as tools hanging on the horn wall flew out from the wall during a blast. The four-foot cone-shaped horn was positioned high in the apex through the wall at the rear of the building. It was made from half-inch cast iron. The large end was twenty inches in diameter. At the cone's smaller end was a five-inch-diameter slotted cylinder and piston. The movement of the piston caused pressurized air to vibrate it and produce a distinctive two-toned blast ending with a grunt, different from a ship's monotone horn.

Occasionally, in freezing weather, condensation produced by the warm compressed air froze and blocked the piston. The diaphone would have to be taken apart, the ice cleared out and the device reassembled. When there was a malfunction of either light or horn that would impair them for more than a few minutes, we had to send a radio message so that the marine radio could notify mariners that this particular light station was inoperative. To work quickly, under pressure, with primitive tools, required ingenuity and calm concentration.

The compressed air (30 psi) was stored in two tanks twelve feet long, six feet in diameter. We had to check the gauges and pump up the tanks regularly—usually once a day—so that the engine equipment would be instantly ready should the fog roll in. That happened

From the beach at Lennard Island, the view of the light tower was beautiful, especially on a nice day. The cluster of three lightkeepers' homes can be seen at left, behind a thicket of salal.

frequently and quickly during fog season, late summer and fall. As well, the horn and other equipment had to be kept well oiled and in good working condition at all times.

The newest addition to the engine house was two Lister diesel engines that drove two power generators to produce 5 kilowatts of electricity. When we arrived, the electric power was on four hours a day for the houses and engine room, but the main light in the tower would not be installed for another two weeks. Five kilowatts was a paltry amount of power considering that three families and a light station were sharing it. Use of the two engines was alternated daily so that any maintenance such as oil changes and adjustments could be done.

The engine house faced the restless open Pacific Ocean at one end of an elevated wooden ramp 250 feet long. At the other end was the winch and loading platform for supplies. Halfway along was the back door to our house, and directly in front of the door was a short ramp leading to the tower. Nestled fifteen feet below in the clearing, one on either side of our house, were two new bungalows. Each of these had a living room, two bedrooms, kitchen with a new wood and coal stove and a basement, half of which was a water cistern.

Now that the station was wired for electricity, the senior keeper moved the AM battery-operated radio to one of the bedrooms in his house where it could be used with an electric transformer. The radio had been in the engine room powered by a large, heavy, cumbersome lead acid battery that needed recharging regularly with a small generator. It was more convenient for him to have it in his house, but he restricted any use of it for the other keepers, except to report local weather on their shift. Over a twenty-four-hour period the keepers produced many weather reports consisting of wind velocity and direction, amount of cloud cover, precipitation and visibility (including the type of restriction, such as fog or drizzle) and condition of sea—calm, rippled, choppy, moderate or rough. It was uncomfortable for Trev to enter the senior keeper's home during the night shift and go through to the bedroom to give the weather report.

Many people have asked us over the years, "What does a light-keeper do?"

Trev was handed a manual as we set out for our first lightstation, and we still have this priceless fount of information: *Rules and Instructions for Lightkeepers and Fog Alarm Engineers and Rules Governing Buoys and Beacons*. It was printed "by the authority of the Department of Transport, Ottawa, Canada" in 1953 and it began with a note:

> These Rules and Instructions are issued by the Department of Transport to be observed by all Lightkeepers and Fog Alarm Engineers in the skilful and faithful performance of their *important duties upon which greatly depends the security of the life and property engaged in navigation.* (My emphasis.)

The primary duty of the lightkeeper was to maintain and operate the light and the foghorn. Under the chapter "Exhibition of Lights" in the manual:

> 6. No circumstance whatever will excuse any keeper for failure to properly exhibit the light or lights in his charge at the prescribed time or for neglecting to keep them burning with the greatest possible brilliancy.

And under the section titled "Lightkeepers in Charge of Mechanically Operated Fog Alarms":

> 3. Failure to act promptly and as befits a man of ordinary skill and good judgment will not be excused, should any unforeseen condition arise which is not covered by these regulations.

The manual goes on to note in exquisite detail rules under the headings of "Light Attendance," "Care and Maintenance of Lights and Apparatus," "Repairs," "Painting," "Care and Handling of Stores," "Fire Precautions" and "General."

It was interesting to note, under the heading "General":

> In addition to their regular routine duties, keepers must at all times be ready to perform any duties connected with the repair of the lighthouses or apparatus, maintenance of lights, preservation of stores, repairing and keeping in order dwelling houses, landing places, roads, drains, fences and everything belonging to the Department; in short, a keeper is expected to take the same care of his station and do the same work about it, as a thrifty man would do with his own property.

And in Part 11, Lightkeepers in Charge of Mechanically Operated Fog Alarms, were such headings as Oil and Engine Driven Plants, Maintenance of Machinery in General and Other Specialized Equipment. There was even a section for the operation of Hand Foghorns and Bells, Mechanical Bells, Radio Phone and Radio Beacons and Rules Governing Buoys, and finally rules governing landing storage and use of oils and fuels at government lightstations, fog alarms and depots. In other words, the duties of lightkeepers were all-encompassing.

Duty was omnipresent, but sometimes we could combine duty with pleasure. I was not keen about heights, but Trev persuaded me to go with him to the top of the tower on his last windup. The lightkeeper on duty was supposed to wind the weight to the very top so that the relieving lightkeeper would not have to begin his shift by doing this task. On stormy nights one could feel the whole tower swaying, and the view from the lantern was magnificent as the lighthouse beam flashed on spray flung high—probably a hundred feet above the monstrous waves.

It was December and the west coast winter storms had begun in earnest. The storms fascinated us. We would stand for hours on the rocks watching the action. One day we were out taking pictures of a wild storm and I just had to get down lower for a better perspective, when suddenly I was inundated with water! Trev stood on a rock just above me, doubled over, laughing so hard he could not snap the picture. It could have been very serious, however. If the true wave, not just the spray, had caught me, I would have been swept out to sea. We gained much respect for the sea and its power. We stand in awe to this day.

The search for firewood seemed never-ending. Trev noticed that logs were more likely to be around during a storm so there he would be, matching wits with the sea, to snag a good log or two and anchor them on shore for future cutting. Gradually he got a little ahead so that the cut wood sometimes had a few days to dry in the wind.

Meanwhile, back in the kitchen, I was still locked in battle with that dilapidated stove. The wood seldom had time to dry properly, I could not manage the damper to control the temperature with the variable winds, and the oven door still had to be propped shut with a stick of wood. Fortunately, we had brought along our Coleman camp stove, which we used for most of the stove-top cooking.

I had never baked bread, but it seemed the only way to keep a month's supply of bread in our third of the 17-cubic-foot freezer. Not that we enjoyed using it. The freezer was stored in the senior keeper's basement, which meant we had to carry huge amounts of frozen foods between houses. My first attempts at baking were dismal failures. I had so carefully followed the recipe, wrapped the dough container in blankets and put it behind the stove to rise. I had coaxed the fire to produce enough heat for baking, but after the bread was in the oven the temperature dropped as the fire fizzled, and there the dough sat, not rising or browning! Little bricks! Eventually I became more expert at making the bread dough and more adept at keeping the fire going. Drier wood also helped.

It seemed I was forever baking bread. Two teenaged boys required constant stoking and we just couldn't fill those boys, especially Garry. He was sixteen when we came to Lennard Island, five-foot-three and wiry. As he stuffed the bread and pancakes and anything handy into his mouth, we noticed a marked change as his cheeks filled out and he even acquired a bit of a belly. Then, suddenly, he started to grow and grow and grow. He grew nine inches in nine months. Even the twenty-six loaves I baked every week seemed inadequate to provide the fuel for this growth.

With electricity and water restricted, the family wash had to be done at night, the only time power was turned on because it was needed for the main light. I did the laundry in the bathroom, and it required a lot of pumping with the hand pump! I could rinse the clothes in the bathtub but there was nowhere to hang them to dry inside the house. Outside was impossible—it was either raining or blowing a hurricane. Finally Trev suggested we dry the clothes in the attic of the engine room. The clothes did dry beautifully there, but we had to carry heavy baskets of wet clothes more than a hundred yards on the elevated ramp, often struggling against the wind.

On one of my expeditions to the engine house attic, I noticed a small pot-bellied iron stove. I thought to myself, Now wouldn't that make a splendid cookie jar for all those hundreds of cookies I make to feed the hungry kids. Trev thoughtfully scraped it down to bare metal, inside and out, polished the outside and painted the inside for my Christmas present. We put the now shining black stove in a corner of the big old kitchen, stuck a philodendron plant in the chimney hole, and tried to keep it full of cookies.

Christmas was fast approaching. Somehow it had not occurred to

By Christmas 1961, we had made Lennard Island a warm and cozy home. The crew on the lifeboat from Tofino braved inclement weather to bring our Christmas turkey and a few special gifts for the children. The glass ball on the mantlepiece was made by Trev, from fragments of a broken Japanese fishing float he had found on the beach.

us to prepare for the holiday before we moved to the station. In any case, we would not have had time. We hoped to send out for some presents by mail, but the lifeboat was not able to come every Friday as had been indicated in our information. Sea conditions do not always obey regulations. So we got busy making things. I made memory candles for our families and friends, decorated with shells from the beaches. These candles I hoped everyone would light on Christmas day, thinking of each other although we were miles apart. Finally the lifeboat was able to make the trip from Tofino, safely enter the gap and offload the turkey we had ordered and a special doll for wee Adrienne. I made cards for friends from some of the coloured paper we had purchased for Adrienne's kindergarten course. In spite of primitive conditions, lack of festive supplies and visiting friends, I remember that first Christmas with a glow: the house in order, plenty of baking prepared, turkey for the table and a roaring fire in the fireplace. The cards, parcels and letters from friends had never meant so much as they did that year—we didn't feel so alone. Even though we couldn't pop over to a friend's for a visit or have people drop in to see us face to face, there was much to be thankful for.

Of course we were not really alone on Lennard Island. The other junior keeper and his wife seemed friendly enough, and they had a daughter a little older than Adrienne who often joined in with our kindergarten activities. I thought the arrangement should be more reciprocal, but I didn't know how to suggest it.

The senior keeper, on the other hand, had one of the foulest mouths I had ever heard, so I tried to keep the children close to the hearth. We caught only occasional glimpses of his wife as she flitted outside briefly. Their bedroom blind was often drawn for days on end. I wondered if she was not well, but I had too much to contend with in our own house to worry about it, and the keeper did not mention anything to us. He had his own speedboat and went to Tofino frequently. He would lower his boat to the water with the hook and cable and row out to it in a small dinghy, leaving the dinghy tied to the hook for his return. There was also an old clinker-built station boat, but it was not serviceable and the motor needed repair. There was no possible way we could go for any provisions or mail in Tofino. So, apart from the irregular stops of the lifeboat, we depended on the senior keeper and his dashes to Tofino to take our mail. But we never knew when that would be. Most times he would leave on the spur of the moment without telling us, and we would see him flash past our window and out to his boat.

Nor did we know when he would come back. He might return the same day, and then again he might not. When he did return the same day, he was often in his cups. One day he went racing off to Tofino and returned under the influence. A slight chop had come up during his absence and the very small dinghy had taken on a goodly amount of water. He fastened his boat to the hook and attempted to board the dinghy, but in his tipsy condition, he lost his balance and fell. This submerged one end of the dinghy and completely filled it with water. The keeper managed to scramble back into his boat and with some effort bailed most of the water out of the dinghy. He then got back in, this time carefully sitting in the middle, and cast off and rowed for shore. The dinghy sat very low in the water and the slight chop brought more water over the side. As each slop washed into the dinghy, it sank lower and lower in the water until finally it was completely submerged. There he was, frantically oaring his submerged craft, his body in the water up to his armpits. Trev raced to the boathouse, grabbed some rope and scrambled down the cliff to a point where he could throw the keeper a line. Finally, after much difficulty, Trev pulled him ashore, so spent from effort and exposure he was unable to climb the cliff. Trev half-carried, half-dragged him over the rocks to the winch house. It was a hilarious incident that could have been tragic.

Now, without a dinghy, the senior keeper was unable to get to his boat once he let it down the cable to the water. He and the other keepers rigged a complex system where one man would work the winch to let the cable go slack while another man pulled the cable and boat toward shore. This way they could bring his boat near enough to shore for him to get on or off.

One day not long after, the keeper returned, again under the influence, and the men began the involved procedure to get him ashore. The other junior keeper worked the winch to let the cable go slack and Trev was down on the rocks at the edge of the cliff hauling the steel cable to bring the boat to shore. He had it within about fifteen feet when the keeper staggered up onto the bow, yelling, "I can make it, I can make it!" And walked right off into the water. He couldn't swim, so Trev hauled him out again and packed him up the cliff to the house.

Another night he had not returned from Tofino by the time Trev finished the evening shift, so we went to bed. We were sound asleep in the front bedroom when suddenly I woke with a start, light blazing in my eyes and an apparition bending over the bed yelling, "Trev, Trev, the belt's broke, the belt's broke!" I clutched the blankets around my neck as Trev rolled out of bed and went with the other junior keeper.

As it turned out, the junior keeper could simply have started the other engine and left the belt repair for later. That was all Trev did. There were no locks on any of our doors, but he also made sure there was a knife in our back door before getting back into bed. This knife also took care of the senior keeper's annoying habit of flinging open our door without knocking, at any time, and walking in.

For all I knew, characters and incidents like this were quite usual in lighthouses, logging camps and similar "rough" outdoor situations. But for me, they only added to the stress. I found more and more that I couldn't cope. There just seemed too much to fit into any one day. It was difficult for Trev to get any sleep after being on a midnight shift with the household so busy during the day. And I found it trying to take care of all the household work with constant interruptions from three teenagers and a preschooler with school questions. Like the time I kept adding salt to the bread batter while answering some query and then wondered why the batter wouldn't rise until I happened to taste it. What to do? We couldn't afford to waste that much food. The only solution was to keep adding flour, fat and water until the salt taste was reasonable. I might add that I was up the rest of the day and following night in the bake shop—loaves of bread galore, buns, cinnamon buns, more bread, sweet bread, coffee bread. It was some of the best baking I had done, and no more baking for a day or two!

But finally, we had to sit down and take stock.

I decided to cut out all extras—like making the kids clothes. They did not need as many nor as fashionable for this life anyway. I could continue to unravel sweaters and knit the extra warm socks needed in that cold house. I could do that while discussing school problems and supervising studies. We also realized that we did not need to conform to "society's" habits of time. We would find it much easier to go with the flow of this life. It just wasn't necessary to have the children begin their school day at 9:00 a.m. as I kept trying to do. Trev had been alternating evening and midnight shifts with the other junior keeper. We decided that Trev would ask to take the midnight shift permanently and the family would all go on shift with him, starting our day at midnight. This worked better than we had supposed. We would all go to bed about 2:00 in the afternoon, get up about 11:00 p.m. and have our breakfast. Trev then took up his duties and the children began their lessons for the day. The generator would be on all night to supply power to the main light so I could use all the electric appliances in my domestic duties. There were no wonderful distractions during the night, such as the arrival of the lifeboat, so school work was finished in record time and come morning our family was free for exploration and relaxation.

By March we were finally settling into a routine of work and play, and life was more regular. But Stan's teeth were really bothering him, and I knew I would have to take him to Victoria to our dentist. The lifeboat came for us. From Tofino we took the bus over the "new" road to Port Alberni, which was really only a patchwork of narrow gravel logging roads, rough with potholes and sharp jagged rocks. As the bus climbed seventeen hundred feet up and over the mountain switch-backs I looked outside with fright. We were terrifyingly close to the edge, and I could see nothing between us and valleys hundreds of feet below, not even guard rails to give the illusion of protection. In Victoria, I took the opportunity to pack Trev's chain saw and other tools, which had been stored at my parents' house, to bring back with me on the bus. I also arranged to have our trusty, well-made Peterborough canoe sent up on the next tender. This canoe had been especially designed for Trev's fishing expeditions in Ontario. It was shorter and wider so that he could comfortably portage it by himself.

Meanwhile, the personnel manager at the Department of Transport found out I was in town and phoned me. He chatted a while—aimlessly, it seemed to me—asking about the family and how we were making out. Then he finally asked me to come to the office for a visit. I had steered clear of the office, leaving that part of our life in Trev's hands, but I thought a specific request could not be ignored. At the office, he again chatted away and then asked me if I had seen the form which was sent to all lightkeepers once each year wherein they were asked to give a spiel about themselves and list any lightsta-tion positions they would be interested in for promotion or transfer. This procedure likely began before there was reliable radio communi-cation, when lightkeepers depended on mail by boat which could take six months or more, and was not changed once faster ways to contact lightkeepers were introduced. Thus the normal civil service proce-dure—to notify employees as each vacancy occurred so that they could apply for it—was not applied to lightstations. Instead, the selection board used the annual list of preferences filled in by each

Food and other supplies were brought to Lennard and other lightstations by the supply ship. A workboat then took the crates in closer to the island and attached them to the cable in a bonnet sling (hanging from cable) so that they could be winched to a loading platform on shore.

lightkeeper to offer vacant positions to eligible lightkeepers at intervals during the year. Trev had mentioned something, I said, but I had not paid much attention, having other things on my mind. He said, "Do you know how many positions he had listed?" (There were spaces for five, but one could add more on the back, if desired.)

"No," I said, "I have no idea."

He replied, "He listed forty-five!"

Having had many years' experience with government bureaucracies, Trev had reasoned that if he listed every position above Lennard Island, then if any became vacant, he would have a chance at being selected for the position.

We had quite a chuckle a couple of months later when the following letter was sent to all lightkeepers from the District Marine Agent in Victoria:

Re: Annual Promotion Competition

There have been requests, during the past few weeks, to be considered for stations other than those shown on the list submitted in conjunction with the annual canvas. Your attention is drawn to the fact that you have only one opportunity for vacancies which arise during that year. The only change would be in the case of a new position being established.

You should ensure that the list submitted annually, contains all the positions to which you would be interested in being moved. If you feel that a move is imperative then you should make certain that you have listed a sufficient number of positions, keeping in mind that many employees may be looking for a promotion to a higher classification or a transfer to a more desirable location.

Requests to be considered for positions not included on the list submitted at the beginning of the calendar year will not be entertained.

Each lightstation was classified from one to nine, nine being the highest pay. One to six positions were usually junior positions. The class depended on the function, equipment and degree of isolation. For instance, Race Rocks, class eight, was a first class light with a radio beacon and foghorn, and the keeper there gave local weather seven times in a twenty-four-hour period. McInnis Island, with the same equipment and duties but with the added duty of synoptic weather and a higher isolation factor, was a class nine.

When we joined the service in 1961, the department was placing three lightkeepers on each station so that they would only have to work eight hours a day, rather than twelve. We understood the plan was to increase the number to four men so that keepers could also indulge in free weekends, like any other civil servant. This plan never materialized. As a matter of fact, over the years, the number of lightkeepers on a station was gradually reduced to two.

By now spring was nosing its way in and work went ahead at a greater pace. We all pitched in to help Trev build up our wood supply for the next winter. The chain saw made such a difference. The boys helped their dad saw and chop while the girls and I stacked.

The trail around the island developed more quickly now with the advent of the chain saw to cut away fallen trees. Every day a new delight was discovered: a rugged ravine rank with wild west coast growth—fir trees, salal, moss and craggy rocks washed by clear powerful

One of our favourite pastimes was gathering up the beautiful shells that washed in along the beaches, and creating special objects for family and friends. Trev's signature pieces were these wonderful "beach birds," welcome lighthearted relief from the challenge of daily life on Lennard Island.

swells, or a closed cove, piled high with battered and bleached logs thrown upon the shore in a fierce storm.

Eventually we came to a deep, narrow gorge completely separating the main island from a smaller one. The boys had discovered it earlier and had been jumping across this dangerous strip. It was just narrow enough for them to make the jump, but one slip on the steep, slippery, rocky sides could be the end in that rushing cold water. Not wanting to ask the boys to stop such tempting sport and knowing they would likely continue to take chances anyway, Trev decided to make a bridge by falling one of the large fir trees across the gorge. He chose the tree carefully and felled it perfectly, trimmed the branches and made it into a safe, sturdy bridge. The senior keeper, on one of his infrequent walks, found the bridge and told Trev to cut it out because it was unsafe. We were green at the job and Trev felt it was his duty to co-operate, so he cut it out. He did build another bridge, though, a splendid one made by securing two smaller logs across the chasm and spiking heavy rough 2x12 boards (snatched from the sea) to the two logs, making a level and firm footing across the gorge. He then made a handrail by securing

*Adrienne enjoys our "private beach" at Lennard Island, spring 1962.
Isolation is one of the challenges of life at a lightstation, but sometimes
it can be a real advantage.*

a cable into the rocks on either end and firmly attaching the cable to
posts he had fastened at intervals the length of the bridge.

This bridge gave us access to joys we had not anticipated. At the
farthest reaches of this tiny island we found a hidden sheltered cove
with a beautiful sparkling white shell beach lapped by gentle surf. This
secluded beach, hard to find and reach, provided a kind of delightful
privacy, far from all the turmoil and cares on the main island. We
often took a picnic lunch and relaxed while Adrienne ran and
splashed in the sea.

One day I noticed that as if by magic the entire hill in front of
our house and down from the tower was covered with a mass of bloom-
ing daffodils! What a heart-lifting sight. It was still early spring with
storms yet to come when these brave blooms poked their heads above
the snow and waved in the wind. Later we found out they had been
planted by Mr. and Mrs. Stout, previous lightkeepers.

One calm, drizzly spring night Trev came in to tell us of an amazing happening. In the beams of the revolving light he had seen what
looked like snow but was really thousands of birds on their migratory

flight north, attracted somehow to the light. We went out to look and saw them hitting the glass of the lantern. Trev and the children went up and gathered the stunned birds, and we collected more from around the base of the tower. That night we had thirty-five different kinds of birds in our kitchen, from a tiny orange crowned warbler to a frightened Canada goose. We examined them carefully in hand, a rare opportunity, and when the birds revived, we released them to continue their flight. What an extraordinary avian experience.

March arrived bright and sunny with the *Camsell* heaving into sight. Soon we saw the helicopter take off and land on our helicopter pad. The Captain and Chief Engineer strolled up to our house carrying a cage. In the cage was Lucky, our cat, who had been left with my parents. Evidently Beth had written to her grandfather saying how they missed their pet, and my father had set about making a sturdy cage with the cat's name prominently painted on the outside. He found out when the next tender was leaving and delivered the cat personally into the hands of the Captain with the urgent request to deliver it to his granddaughter at Lennard Island. So he did!

That cat was a very special cat with a remarkable history. Years before at Miracle Beach—midway between Courtenay and Campbell River on Vancouver Island, where we had lived while Trev completed his final tour with the air force at Comox—I had returned home to find Trev sitting on the sofa with a sheepish look on his face. I plied him with questions until he reluctantly opened his hand to reveal a bit of black fluff in his palm. He had been mowing the lawn, heard a faint mew, and bent down to find this tiny bit of life, eyes still shut and weighing no more than a feather. Trev is not overly fond of cats because they catch and kill birds, his special interest. But here was this puny kitten and what else could we do but keep him? The kids named him Lucky, lucky to be alive. I doubt that he would have lived another day otherwise. Time passed and he grew and flourished with all the lavish attention. When he was only weeks old, he proved his worth by nailing a mouse scooting into the kitchen. He won Trev over when he showed his ineptitude in catching birds. We watched him tensely stalking blue jays, his fluffy Persian tail waving high in the air as a warning flag. The birds took great delight in enticing him. They would hop just a little closer, keeping a wary eye out, then fly off as he prepared to leap.

Some time later, Lucky earned his name again. With nice weather at Miracle Beach I decided to put him out at night, and some old toms mauled him. Our house was near the Provincial Park border. People often lost their pets while camping or left them deliberately, and they became quite wild. I went past the children's bedroom in the morning to see four pairs of reproachful eyes staring at me! They had found Lucky more dead than alive. They reluctantly caught the early school bus and left poor Lucky lying on the bed, not moving. He did not move for days. Finally he stirred and eventually fully recovered, but his black Persian fur had turned silver.

He went everywhere with us. When we camped, he reconnoitred the area to find a convenient high perch where he kept watch. He went along with us in the canoe and even swam on occasion. Now he was at Lennard Island. He and the children were overjoyed.

Only a month later, tragically, Lucky was poisoned and suffered a slow and painful death. We were heartbroken as well as angry and bewildered because we had a suspicion he had been deliberately poisoned. Why would anyone murder our beloved pet?

The loss of Lucky was softened somewhat as we found new interest and adventure with the canoe and motor that had come on the same tender as our unlucky feline. Rationally I knew that fragile craft with a half-horsepower motor could be used only under ideal conditions on this treacherous coast, but psychologically I was no longer trapped. In the months that followed, we spent many interesting and profitable hours with the canoe. Trev caught cod and salmon now and then, a welcome addition to our dinner table. We had much more freedom to observe wildlife. One splendid day when the swells smoothed and were not breaking, we were even able to circumnavigate nearby Echachis Island.

In March and April we saw whales blowing about a mile offshore and identified them as gray whales. Trev wrote to the Biological Station. They were doing a study on the gray whale migration up the west coast and they asked Trev to become a whale watcher, keeping records of numbers, activity and location. This proved to be a very

One spring night in 1962, thousands of birds on their flight north were somehow confused by the light beams from the tower and began hitting the glass. We brought many of the stunned birds into the kitchen—we counted thirty-five different species!—and released them as they recovered.

interesting part of our life as we watched the whales following the shore quite closely on their northward journey. One day we were able to observe two massive gray whales mating directly below the winch house. What a sight! Two huge whales, like tanker trucks, copulating belly to belly, and in one flash it was over. Others would raise half their body length from the water and vigorously slap back down. We wondered whether they were trying to dislodge some of the accumulation of barnacles adhering to their hides, or playing, exercising, communicating or courting.

Another day Trev and the boys were clambering over the rocks when they spotted a bedraggled oil-soaked bird. They brought it to the house and after many cleanings we recognized it as a California murre. The murre is about a foot long with a white breast and grey back, and it walked erect, much like a penguin. We could not let this one loose as we knew his natural oil had been washed away with the various cleaning processes. He became a member of our household for a while. The children spent a lot of time capturing bullheads and small fish for his food. They put the fish, alive and swimming, in a basin placed in front of the bird. With lightning stabs of his bill, he killed them all and then devoured them. Just as quickly they came out the other end! Now, on top of all my other duties, I was carrying a roll of toilet paper under my arm. The murre rapidly lost its appeal for me.

But he did have a personality and took a real fancy to Adrienne, following on her heels wherever she went. We had to be sure that the kitchen door to the living room and her bedroom was shut securely at night or he would appear at her bedside, having squirted a trail as he went. Finally, we decided he had preened enough oil onto his feathers for protection. Trev led the expedition to the beach for his release. The murre started out with great fanfare, swimming straight for the open ocean. We could see him sinking lower and lower in the water. Then he turned about and headed right back to us. Unfortunately, the cold water had gotten through to his skin and chilled him. He developed pneumonia a few days later and didn't survive.

One day my greatest fear was realized. I was preparing some baking in the large old pantry, and Trev was talking to the senior keeper, who was perched on a stool in our kitchen, looking every bit like Popeye with his cap on his head, his pipe dangling from a corner of his mouth, and his eyes squinting. Suddenly I heard a piercing wail from outside and instinctively knew it was terribly serious. Before I had crossed the kitchen on the way to the back door, Beth flew through the door to me, her right hand clutching her left. I lifted it to look in horror at what seemed like a severed hand with blood gushing out. I immediately turned to the keeper and asked him to call the lifeboat. He casually got off the stool and started sauntering over to me, drawling, "Now, Mrs. Anderson, let's have a look."

Cold fury raced from my toes up my back, perhaps similar to what a mother bear feels when protecting her young. I felt that if he stood there one second longer, watching my little girl bleed to death, I would cheerfully strangle him. He must have recognized something in my deadly still voice and clenched teeth, as I looked straight at him and quietly breathed, "Get the lifeboat!" On our house radio we heard his voice breaking through as he called Tofino radio.

Meanwhile, Trev sat Beth down, elevated her arm and held a compress on her gashed hand. Even so, the basin below was filling with blood. It seemed we spent hours watching her get paler and paler and begin to shake before the boys ran in to tell us the lifeboat was entering the gap. We whipped Beth into a warm sleeping bag and Trev marched, with the longest strides I've ever seen him take, to the little beach. A crew member from the lifeboat was heading in with a small skiff. A big sea was running, but thank goodness the crewman was handling the dinghy as if he was a part of it. Expertly he brought the skiff through the gap to the beach on a big swell, and Trev seemed to walk on water as he strode across rocks and into the skiff without slowing down. They were soon aboard the lifeboat and on the way to Tofino.

Later I found out Beth had got to the hospital in Tofino faster than if we had been in a city—it took less than an hour. Trev settled her in the hospital and then had to return to his duties at the lightstation. Then began the long wait, not knowing what was happening. We reasoned she must be all right or we would have been notified, but it was agony. There was no way to visit her and we had no telephone or radio transmitter of our own.

Finally, days later, we saw the lifeboat heading for Lennard Island, and as it came nearer we saw Beth in the wheelhouse with the coxswain. There was quite a sea running and they had to turn and head back to Tofino. When she was safely home a few days later, she told us that the coxswain had talked to the senior keeper on the radio and told him to tell us he was bringing her out. Later he had radioed again and told him to tell us that he was returning her to the hospital until better conditions prevailed for landing. We never received these messages from the senior keeper. We later heard that the coxswain had lost a daughter to drowning when she was just about Beth's age. He wasn't about to take any chances with this young girl.

The doctor, Dr. McDiarmid, had done a magnificent job on her hand. All the tendons on top of her hand had been cut, but luckily, not the underside. These he carefully stitched together along with other repairs. She was in a cast for many weeks. When we went in to have the cast removed, he gave us a course of therapy treatments which we religiously carried out. Her hand eventually healed with no loss of strength or dexterity.

After things settled down, we found out how the accident had happened. She and the boys were clearing salal from their play area. Garry was handling the machete and Beth reached in to clear some branches just as he swung. Stan said adrenalin sure must have been working as Beth didn't go the long way round, she just sped lightly right on top of the dense salal, screaming for Mom as she clutched her hand. Poor Garry walked the beach alone, afraid to come in, more afraid that he had cut off her hand.

Just recently Beth told me that when the coxswain had turned back, he had not taken her back to the hospital but to Mrs. Sloman, who had been a pupil of my father's long ago. That dear kind lady had pampered Beth every day by bringing her breakfast in bed (her favourite poached egg on toast) and, before she went to sleep at night, a cup of hot chocolate, another special treat.

It wasn't long before we ordered a Heathkit marine band receiver. Trev's air force radio training and knowledge stood him in good stead as he masterfully fitted together the many intricate bits, and soon had the radio working. Now we could tune into the lighthouse frequency and never again fail to receive messages intended for us.

Life was back to normal, and we missed our friends dreadfully although the isolation was broken by a few rare and treasured visitors now that it was summer. We became acquainted with Mr. Stout, the previous lightkeeper, when he came near, threw a salmon ashore and exchanged pleasantries with us. He and his wife were originally from the Orkney Islands in Scotland. Over time they became dear and valued friends and were always there for us when we were in crisis.

My mother, father and uncle managed to come for a weekend when my uncle drove up from California with his pink Cadillac, which they could drive over the new road to Tofino. I believe they had a couple of flat tires travelling that rocky road. Another time, some friends from Miracle Beach chartered a boat in Tofino so that they could visit us for a couple of days. I doubt that anyone who hasn't lived such an isolated life could imagine how much these contacts with friends meant. They renewed our badly bruised spirits.

Early one Saturday morning, the lifeboat, with my cousin and his wife aboard, appeared in the gap. We had no inkling anyone was on the way and we were overjoyed to see them. They weren't exactly attired for clambering out onto slippery rocks, Fay in her high heels and dainty clothes, but we soon had them in lighthouse duds, out exploring the island.

That same day, the senior keeper and his wife took off for Tofino in their boat, and returned later, both of them three sheets to the wind. They were helped up the cliff with great difficulty. The keeper insisted on releasing the cable himself, although his judgement was greatly impaired. He let the cable drop too quickly, which allowed the pulley to go over the side of the boat. When tension was applied to commence lifting, the cable came off the shackle and jammed. Now the boat was partly out of the water and could be neither raised nor lowered. We still had no dinghy, and now we could not lower the station boat, even in a real emergency. We were trapped on that island.

Having witnessed all this, Fran and Fay wanted to leave immediately, but there was no transportation other than the lifeboat, which wasn't due to pick them up until Monday. Trev and Fran went for a walk around the island while Fay and I caught up on months of gossip and I kneaded yet another batch of bread. Trev returned, but without my cousin. A fish boat had passed close to the island towing a dinghy, so he had hailed it and hitchhiked a ride to Tofino, saying he was going to get transportation and come back for his wife. Fay wasn't unduly concerned. We settled down for a good long visit.

Before long, we heard Tofino radio break in on our house radio for the weather, and then they asked whether the keeper had his boat off the hook yet! Within moments we heard the sound of rapid heavy stomping up the stairs at the side of our house. Our door was flung open and the keeper stood there demanding, "Who told Tofino radio about my boat?!"

Trev and Fay were sitting at the table and I was standing in front, kneading my bread. No one spoke. The silence lengthened. Finally I said, "I guess Fran told them."

"Fran, Fran, where is Fran?" he yelled.

More silence. But I couldn't keep my big mouth shut. "He went to Tofino," I said.

He turned to me and snarled, "How did he get to Tofino?"

I had had enough. I put my head down and vigorously went about the job of punching bread. The silence dragged on. Finally Trev looked at him and drawled, "He must have swum, I guess." The keeper looked stunned for a moment, then wheeled around and stomped down the stairs.

At that time the salary for the junior lightkeeper's position—all positions, for that matter—was pathetic, even for the 1960s. Trev's salary was $3,200 a year, and after deductions we were left with about $180 a month! Slim pickings, indeed. So that first spring we turned our thoughts to making a garden. We knew little of gardening, but sent away for books, seeds and fertilizer. Trev dug up some of the big valley between the tower and the engine room, and we planted potatoes. In a patch behind the house we tilled the soil and planted other vegetables. The other junior keeper started another garden near their house and the island hummed with activity.

The senior keeper, too, could be seen reluctantly spading in front of their house. One day I was doing the dishes in the pantry and there he was, busily planting seeds as his small terrier followed along behind, just as busily digging them up. The keeper turned, saw what was happening and with a roar, shovel in hand, took off after the dog. The two of them tore around and around the house, loud curses filling the air. Then their front door opened and the keeper's wife poked her head out the door and whispered, "Here Spot, here Spot!" The dog slipped inside, the door closed gently and the keeper kept going around, uttering oaths and swinging the shovel.

Such bizarre and humorous moments raised our spirits. So did the warmer weather, but it also brought more frequent spells of sea fog. We would see a fog bank far out on the ocean and actually watch it roll rapidly across the sea toward shore. The lightkeeper reacted instantly by racing to the engine room to crank the fog engine and start the air compressor. Soon the deep blare of the foghorn began reverberating miles away through the blanketing mist, warning fish boats and other vessels away from danger. In this warm, moist season the deafening blast rent the air constantly. From atop the tower in the bright blue sky, we could see a blanket of cotton batten covering the sea for miles, with occasional tips of masts poking up through the downy white layer as fish boats plied the waters beneath. On a clear day, boats could be seen fifteen miles offshore fishing over an underwater bank at the extreme outer limit of the horn's range. One day Trev counted more than two hundred on the bank. These boats depended on the familiar blast of the foghorn to guide them safely home. They were a down-to-earth reminder of the need for vigilance in keeping the horn operating in fog. Years later, when Beth was in grade ten, she wrote this essay:

TRUST

"Follow me."

Gingerly I stepped over a rotten log and began a stumbling walk down the narrow path toward the sea. My brother, lean and strong, strode over the familiar trail gradually widening the distance between us. Soon I could only see his blonde head and broad shoulders. Desperately, I lengthened my steps and tripped.

"Stan! Stan! Wait for me."

Patiently, he stopped, turned around, and waited for me to catch up. I scrambled over the rocky terrain to where he stood. He took my hand in his larger one.

"Now step where I do."

With bolder steps I continued forward. I could look around now with confidence. Covering the sea was a gigantic field of cotton batten, fog. I could hear, but not see, the gentle washing of the sea swell over the rocks worn smooth through the centuries. The sun, like a halo, peeked through an opening in the blanketed sky and brightened only this small island of ours. How privileged we were.

The sun's generosity transformed the island from a dull patch of wilderness into a dreamlike paradise. I looked back up the path and saw green, luscious grass. Dainty ferns swayed softly and dandelions poked their sunny heads out of the grass. The tips of the firs were misted with fog. Ahead of me, sea pools in the fissures of the rocks shimmered with colour. Red and green anemones, like immature cacti, purple sea urchins, the porcupine of the sea, and rainbowed starfish cluttered the still waters. Our foghorn's blare echoed and bounced through the haze, warning boats of our treacherous waters. To us it boomed a friendly greeting.

"He-e-l-l-o-o-o."

But to the boats at sea it came faintly.

"Go-o-o-a-wa-ay."

Our lighthouse's beam pierced the fog, giving assistance to the foghorn in its vigil.

Stan suddenly aroused himself from the magic spell nature had woven.

"Come on, quick. Quickly, I said."

"What, what's going on, Stan?"

"Don't ask questions and get a move on. We've only got a few minutes."

"For what?"

But my words were lost as we dashed over the rocks.

Abruptly, Stan stopped. We were in front of the engine house. I looked around bewilderedly. Something seemed radically wrong. The sun had disappeared, darkening the sky. The fog was moving in, becoming thicker and surrounding the engine house and lighthouse. No sound but the sea's whisper. Silence. Something was missing. I should be hearing. Hearing what?

"Well?" I asked Stan.

His answer was to put his fingers in his ears and "scrunch up", waiting....

"Stanley Anderson, what's going on? Why are you doing that? TELL ME!"

No reply came, but his lips quirked and his eyes gleamed devilishly. Now I was really suspicious.

"BA-A-A-A-A-R-R-R-O-O-O-O-O-M-M-PH!"

I spun backwards with the foghorn's blast ringing in my ears, rocketing through my head.

Stan stood grinning with his fingers in his ears.

The warmer weather also allowed us to continue extending and improving our trail around the island. We could now go for parklike walks around the perimeter. Our path system had grown to the extent that names were needed. Nicely shaped pieces of driftwood burned with "Trevor's Trail," another announced "Flo's Flop" high on a knoll, a vantage rest spot. One could walk down "Alan's Alley" past "Larry's Leap" (named for our good friend and his son from Miracle Beach) and on by "Garry's Gorge" and across "Beth's Bridge" to "Stan's Stand" and "Pud's Peak" (our family pet name for Adrienne). The discovery of another cove, this one piled high with driftwood, interested us immensely with jumbled masses of odd-shaped bleached logs. During a storm, foam formed over the whole bay, as if it were covered with snow, and salty bits of fluff blew by us with the wind.

The trails opened the interior of the island and led to the discovery of crows' nests. Stan had heard that it was possible to teach crows to talk if training began early, so he asked his father if he and Garry might take two from a nest and try to teach them to talk. Permission received, they chose a nest to watch for the hatching and then set about energetically building an aviary. Way off in the undergrowth, they discovered an old lean-to. We learned months later that this had been built by Mr. Stout when he was lightkeeper at Lennard Island, to use when building his many boats, especially a clinker-built cabin cruiser for his retirement. He had launched it on rollers made from logs, from the lean-to through a slashed trail, 350 feet to the launching beach.

How those boys worked slashing salal, clearing a path to the lean-to, clearing away the debris and installing old trees for perches! They grubbed around more until they found some old chicken wire which they used to enclose the front. It was a magnificent aviary. Finally the big day arrived. The boys climbed a tree, stole two baby crows and took them to their new home, the aviary. Nothing could have had better care. The crows were indeed pampered pets.

Some weeks later, the keeper informed Trev the boys would have to remove the crows from that shed as he wanted to use it to store wood. Stan came to me practically in tears. I said, "Never mind, Stan, perhaps it is for the best. Wild creatures are really not happy caged." Sorrowfully they released the birds. But it did turn out for the best. Those crows very soon found out where Stan did his schoolwork, near a living room window, and perched on the railing outside waiting for him to come out. They followed the boys everywhere, cawing for handouts. Eventually we realized that food put out for them was not touched until all the thirty cousins had been rallied. The boardwalk took on a very messy look. The boys began feeding them at the beach. From then on we could always tell where the boys were by looking for crows circling overhead.

These crows and their relatives were the zaniest creatures. I remember one day when the entire population of Lennard Island stood on the ramp by the loading platform, waiting for the workboat from the tender. The men and boys were in one group talking, the women in another and the girls in another. The crows were arranged above us and imitating the tone of each group. Over the men there was low muttering, over the women, higher-pitched squawks and over the girls, high chirps.

Other times they spent hours playing games. A favourite one: follow the leader in flight carrying a piece of shingle. After a time serving as leader, the lead crow dropped it and another caught it in midair. Then that crow had a turn at being flight leader.

A crow's eye view of the station in early summer showed the progress of our efforts with all the gardens growing, helicopter pad mowed and a large circle of turf removed to reveal the white shell just below the surface. The engine room had been repainted but still needed reshingling. The other two keepers could not bear heights, so the job fell to Trev. He didn't mind. He enjoys good physical work, especially when the results are so visible. He got right at it and had it completed in short order, including the painting. The old cedar shingles he had shovelled from the roof were heaped in a mess at the side of the building. Trev thought, ah-ha, good kindling. The boys started gathering and stacking them in our cellar out of the rain. But the senior keeper told them to stop and leave it for the others. And there the shingles stayed, not used, ever.

Trev's next job was to climb the lighthouse tower and paint the exterior of the tower lantern. One sunny day he was busily scraping and painting when he caught sight of the other two keepers in the cove below, sawing and stacking the two logs Trev had wrested from the sea and anchored to the beach during the last storm. This time there was no talk of sharing the wood.

In spite of these irritations, our family worked at a productive and even keel. We had talked to the children before moving to the lightstation, explaining the new responsibilities expected of them, and had asked for their support and received their enthusiastic co-operation. In one of Beth's early letters, she wrote:

> Every morning we make our beds and then start our chores. My chores are to set the table as soon as I get up. After meals, I do the dishes by myself. [Here she exaggerated.] The boys have to bring two sacks of driftwood up to the house every day. Besides that Stan has to clean the stove grates and Garry has to clean the fireplace. Mum's first cooking experience on the wood and coal stove didn't turn out so nice. She went out to hang up clothes. She told me to keep the stove going so the cake would bake. Well, every few minutes, I shoved more wood in. By the time Mum got back, the heat in the oven was up to six hundred degrees and the cake was charcoal. It wasn't very tasty.

As the balmy summer rolled along, we discovered new delights. A massive bleeding heart bush bloomed forth with hundreds of flowers. Rufous hummingbirds visited the bush, poking their long bills into the centres of flowers to suck up nectar. Because the tiny birds were not disturbed by our presence, we could observe them closely as they hovered. Rose bushes appeared through tangled grass, with a variety of beautiful blooms. Bunches of purple, red, white and yellow rock flowers grew from cracks in the rocks.

The sea underwent a prolonged spell of calm during which Trev and the boys used the canoe for fishing plenty of cod or making expeditions to the nearby islands. The boys were busy with their school-work at night, at least Stan was, and involved with their crows or other adventures during the day. Beth had worked hard completing grade seven and as a reward went to visit her grandparents in Victoria. The garden was prospering and the station had started to gleam with care. Great stacks of split wood were drying in the sun and breeze.

Then, toward the end of August, a feeling of doom saturated my being. For days I could not shake it. I finally told Trev. It was a beautiful

Our home on Lennard Island, seen here from the light tower, was big but not very homemaker-friendly. I washed and rinsed our clothes in the bathroom, with much pushing on the hand pump; then we carried baskets of wet clothes to the engine room attic and hung them to dry.

day, not a ripple on the sea and no ocean swell. To humour me, but also because on some previous occasions my premonitions had been vividly realized, he decided to go to Tofino with our canoe, pick up the mail and phone our folks. He returned shortly and handed me a letter. It was from the Department of Transport, advising him that his appointment was not being confirmed and we would be picked up with the following tender. *We were fired?!*

The bottom seemed to drop out of our world. To have sacrificed so much to attempt a life we felt was very worthwhile, to put up with the isolation and the rustic facilities and the shift work and our strange neighbours on this island, to work so hard for naught, was more than I could bear.

Trev decided to leave immediately for Victoria and demand some explanation. I could not stay on this island with my children, not with these noxious people who must have been responsible for doing this final harm to us. We could not afford to take the family to Victoria, so

Trev arranged for our dear friends the Stouts to take me and the children to their lovely tranquil home. Serenity.

This wonderful couple, now retired, had hacked and cleared a small island in this virgin country, near Tofino, and built a beautiful little home. Just the two of them had cleared the land, built a prefab log house surrounded by a flower garden, built a wharf, boathouse and bridge to the mainland, and planted a large garden there. All this in less than two years and both of them in their sixties. To this amazing couple goes much of the credit for maintaining my sanity during that desperate time.

In Victoria, Trev went straight to the office and was presented with a file of letters written by the senior keeper, none of them with Trev's knowledge. The letters reported that Trev was wrecking the equipment on the station, destroying the island, and not performing his duties. The department had accepted these allegations, although they had in their files Trev's air force records of consistent responsible performance for twenty years.

"Do you believe this?" Trev said. "How could the keeper say I am incompetent and yet leave me alone when he took the other junior keeper with him to Tofino?"

They asked Trev for more details.

"I can give you dates from my diary if that is any help," he said.

He was told to return to the island and say nothing. There would be an investigation.

My cousin Fran drove Trev back to Tofino over the hair-raising logging road. While waiting at the Port Alberni end for the gate to open, they talked with a tourist from Tofino, and when he heard Trev was from Lennard Island, he said, "Say, I believe some people from there were involved in a peculiar incident as we were leaving Tofino. This odd little character staggered down the hill to the wharf where a woman was lolling on the edge, waiting. He loudly swore at her, wanting to know where she had been." The tourist was describing the senior keeper to a T. He went on to say the man and woman had fallen into the boat secured to the dock, untied it, and taken off at full throttle. As the boat zoomed away, the man wrenched the wheel hard over for a turn and the steering cable snapped. The boat roared around in circles as the man, loudly cursing, told the woman to get to the back of the boat and turn off the engine. She fell and lay sprawled in the boat, as the air was rent with foul language and the boat circled around, barely missing the wharf with each turn. Eventually the man managed to crawl to the rear and shut off the motor.

We returned to the island and closed the walls around our family. Our secluded, satisfying family life continued with hard work and enjoyment of the island as we waited for word from the department. In the end Trev was reinstated. The tender came and went without our departure.

The cold war escalated on all sides, until finally the junior keeper locked himself in, refusing to do his shift and sitting in his house at the window. The keeper radioed Victoria for instructions on how to handle the problem. He was told to give the man a written invitation to take his shift and if he still refused, it would be construed as his resignation. He still wouldn't come out of his house. Shortly after, he left the island on the lifeboat with all his effects.

Soon the December tender arrived with a new junior relief keeper. He was a pleasant Scotsman who had been a senior lightkeeper but had resigned, thinking it would be better for his children. His other job prospect had not worked out and he was endeavouring to re-enter the light service. It was obvious he had been informed of the situation on Lennard and was stepping gently. We were very reluctant to extend our trust, but made neighbourly gestures and exchanged visits over Christmas and New Year's. I felt sorry for the family man away from his wife and children at that time of year.

We had barely adjusted to the turmoil of the arrival of a new keeper when I discovered a large lump on the side of my back. I went to Tofino and made the hazardous trip alone by bus over the new road to Victoria. Fortunately the lump was found to be benign, and I was able to return to my family because the doctor gave me instructions for Trev to remove the stitches.

No sooner had that crisis ended than the new relief keeper's family came to join him on the February tender. Our children viewed the arrival of three girls with great excitement and interest. The prospect of other children on the island was a real novelty. Two of the girls were about Beth's age and one a little younger than Adrienne.

The lifeboat from Tofino made regular trips to Lennard Island, and on rare and welcome occasions the boat arrived with guests aboard. To visit us, family and friends had to drive the rough new road across Vancouver Island to Tofino, then make the journey in the lifeboat— weather permitting.

Life settled back into a pleasant routine, the children completing written correspondence assignments and their regular chores quickly so that they could spend more waking hours exploring, playing and getting to know the other youngsters. Beth and Adrienne, although eight years apart, had fun "dressing up." Adrienne was usually the model while Beth dressed her, for instance, in complete regalia as Queen Victoria or as an Indian princess, then took photos with her little Brownie camera to record the event. Adrienne raced around inside the house on her tricycle, back wheels just narrow enough to go through interior door frames, and outside, bumping along the wooden ramp or racing down the seashell path. Beth spent hours by herself, designing paper clothes for Millie the Model (a comic strip character) and designing, knitting and crocheting clothes for a baby doll. They had a farm set and Beth then made a herd of stick horses with elaborately drawn and crayoned cardboard heads. The other toy she treasured was a two-foot-high stuffed poodle—a Christmas present. She even kept socks on its feet to protect it and keep it new-looking.

The boys devised more physical and daredevil pursuits like making bows and arrows with metal arrowheads painted red, and David and Goliath slingshots (one rock barely missed the girls, who were playing in a bedroom as a rock flew through the window and ricocheted around the room). In their cleared "play area," they hung onto a stout rope tied high in a tree and jumped from a log. They gradually developed more and more difficult jumps and made elaborate paper awards for each type of leap onto the salal spring mattress. Beth, although younger and small physically, was allowed to compete for the awards only if she performed at their level!

February, our second on this island, was mostly a sunny crisp month on the west coast. This gave the men an opportunity to get at the outside duties—painting, digging gardens and cleaning up the winter debris left by storms. There was a promise of spring as the daffodils came into bud and the air freshened.

The keeper continued his frequent and impromptu dashes into Tofino. One sunny day after the keeper had spent the night away, a helicopter arrived on the island. It was the office personnel. Soon the keeper returned in his usual inebriated condition and, after a talk with the bosses, he resigned.

The office people then discussed the running of the station until a senior relief keeper arrived. The plan was that he would take charge as soon as possible and stay until a competition could be held to fill the position. They wanted to know if the junior relief and Trev wanted equal responsibility until the senior relief could be brought to the station. Trev suggested that since the other junior had more experience, and it was better to have one person handling the administration, it should be left to him in the interim.

The new senior relief keeper arrived a couple of weeks later, and new tensions sprang up as authority and power were redistributed among the staff. Finally the new senior relief let the junior man know in no uncertain terms who was now in charge, which created ill feeling between the two. Our family was determined to maintain cordial relations with all, and the junior keeper's wife must have felt as we did, for she tried her best to maintain good relations by keeping communication open and taking bits of baking to the senior relief.

For us the new senior man revived a sense of fun that had been missing over these past trying months. We made a point of inviting him to Sunday dinners, which we always tried to keep special. On one trip to Tofino, he heard via local gossip that the former keeper had called Trev "the Duke." The Duke? Well, I, then, must be the Duchess, I said!

So the following Sunday he presented Trev with a most delightful "royal" crown. It must have taken him many, many painstaking hours to put together. Bits of metal soldered into a frame. Red silk, scrounged from the kids, tucked inside and an imitation ermine rim. Sunday dinners took on a regal elegance.

Nothing would do but we had to have a crest. The senior relief keeper designed one portraying Lennard Island with a heavy rain cloud covering the island. (A slight exaggeration on his part!)

The relief keeper was an adamant Conservative. The 1963 federal election campaign was underway, so for argument's sake, Trev took on the Liberal position. One night, Trev went to the engine room to find little paper feet tied to a line leading to a big sign, FOLLOW DIEF. Trev waited until the keeper was asleep and attached a sign to his door, LESTER IS BESTER. Our big old house was built far from the ground on the living room side. The windows could only be reached by ladder. Yet here, one morning on opening the drapes, we found a sign, FOLLOW DIEF. When the time came, the lifeboat took us all to Tofino to vote. Ironically, the senior relief was ineligible to vote as his name had not been transferred from Victoria!

Our morale was definitely boosted by the lighter mood and humour over those few weeks. But the emotional turmoil of the previous months had taken their toll. When Trev was offered a position at Barrett Rock, just outside Prince Rupert, he accepted. It was still a class three, the same as Lennard Island, but a senior keeper's position. We would be moved there with the first available tender going to the northern agency.

It was February 1963, fourteen months since our arrival at Lennard Island, and Trev immediately started partially crating our furniture with the crates he had made in Vancouver. He had made tops and bottoms for each crate. Slats were then easily nailed to tops and bottoms around the sides, leaving the front open so that we could still use each piece of furniture. At the last moment, the front slats could be nailed in place. We packed as many of the rest of our belongings as possible. For months

On a foggy day in early spring, exploring the rich tide pools on the rocky shores of Lennard could be a magical experience.

we lived amidst boxes and wooden containers. Before long, it gave me great satisfaction to give the crates a swift kick as I passed.

Relief from the chaos of packing and the tension of waiting came when Mr. Stout had to go to Victoria for medical treatment. He could not leave Mrs. Stout without a man to help with the boat, their only transportation to Tofino, and he did not want to leave her alone at this isolated spot or to leave their place unattended. They asked us to visit with her while he was away. We had leave coming and we were relieved to get away. What a synchronistic break.

The following ten days were a priceless gift. Stout's island home, about four miles from Tofino along Browning Passage, was almost completely protected from storms. Peace, utter peace. No crashing waves, no tension between people, no continuous fog vigilance. And there was Mrs. Stout, calm, unflappable, an anchor in the storm. The boys and Trev often went fishing with one of the boats while the girls and I enjoyed Mrs. Stout's company. She showed us how she made Scottish scones—kneading on paper so as not to waste any flour—and digging in her huge garden of vegetables and flowers. When the tide was at the lowest ebb, the mud flats in Browning Passage extended as

61

far as the eye could see, softly stretched rolling plains of sand and mud with winding creek beds slicing the flatness into a variety of segments. On first glance I thought I was on the prairies, but this was mud, lots and lots of mud. One day when the tide was out, unbeknownst to me, the girls decided to walk to Tofino. They were unaware of the danger from the incoming tide. Mrs. Stout and I looked out to see my two little daughters away off in the distance, trudging toward civilization. They would occasionally disappear from sight as one of the mud hills hid them from view. The tide, we knew, would soon turn and rapidly fill the channel basin. We called and called but they were too far away to hear. Finally Mrs. Stout phoned the lifeboat in Tofino.

The lifeboat came quickly up the rivulet channels not emptied by the tide. The same engineer who had manoeuvred the dinghy so expertly when Beth was taken to hospital for her cut hand now waded across the last cold, cold water and took the girls to the lifeboat. They had taken a dinghy with them and were dragging it along the tiny rivulets. We did not know this, because the dinghy was always hidden from our view. Nevertheless, they were mighty glad to see the lifeboat, and you may be sure they never tried that again!

Meanwhile, back on Lennard Island, the senior was lazily listening to the radio when he heard that the Tofino lifeboat had rescued the children from Lennard Island. Sure gave him a start!

We returned to Lennard Island relaxed in body and refreshed in spirit. But Garry was restless. Our problems adjusting to the new life had been so overwhelming, we did not recognize Garry's greater need as a sixteen-year-old. He needed to be with his peers. He stoically accepted his share of chores and joined is in our family life, but simply sat obediently at his desk doing nothing. No inducement could get him the least bit interested in his schoolwork. He was behaving exactly like a progressive teenager and didn't know it. Neither did his parents! One time, egged on by his siblings while Trev and I were out slashing trails, he gave himself an Iroquois haircut, using the razor to cut two strips of hair cleanly from his head. This trendsetter also wanted to dye his pants red. I wouldn't dye the pants, but when he went to Victoria, his grandmother obliged! One day we discovered him on the beach preparing to set sail for Tofino in a "boat" he had built from slender laths hastily nailed together and covered with one of my sheets. He had then slapped on a few coats of paint.

Looking back, we realize we should have simply let him set aside the studies for a while and spend his time growing up. But at the time, responsibility for the children's education weighed so heavily I lay awake night after night wondering how to guide him. Finally it occurred to me that the air force might be the solution. There he would have food, shelter, clothing, training and supervision. We did not see the rest of the reality—that he was really still a growing boy, just seventeen, now six feet tall, but barely 130 pounds, and he had never been away from home.

Of course he jumped at the idea—anything to get away from the island where he felt trapped and bored. He was accepted but on the condition he put on some weight. We bought Wate-on, and served up fattening foods. He ate and ate and soon gained enough to be away on his adventure. The stress was just too much for him and the asthma he had had as a baby recurred. Garry was medically discharged from the air force. He did not return to the island. He went to my sister's for a while and she tried to settle him, but he wandered and was a worry for several years before he settled down.

Meanwhile, the Lennard Island station was humming with the arrival of Shell Oil, which was preparing to do underwater exploration work in the Pacific. The men went to the helicopter pad to greet the staff and help unload supplies. As the pilot climbed out of the chopper he turned to Trev and said, "What are you doing here?" It was a pilot from the air force days and Trev was just as surprised to see him.

Two Shell Oil fellows erected a large tent near the helicopter pad and began setting up equipment. The instrument installed in the tent at Lennard Island, the master station, was used to accurately plot by triangulation the position of ships at sea. Two slave stations were located at Cape Beale and Estevan Point. A small power plant outside the tent supplied power to a transmitter that triggered transmission from the slaves. Ships picking up these signals could plot their position very accurately by using other equipment to measure in microseconds the time interval between the three transmissions.

The former senior keeper had arranged to board the two on

Holidays and birthdays were extra-special occasions on Lennard. Above, a gypsy lady and Peter Pan pose for their Halloween portrait, October 1962. Below, our children and the relief lightkeeper's daughters enjoy the carnival they organized in honour of Adrienne's sixth birthday, May 1963.

Lennard Island, but he was gone now and the senior relief had come for a "short interval," bringing only a folding cot and very little gear. He asked me if I could handle boarding the men if they slept in his house with cots and sleeping bags. My pay for boarding the men would be paid by the Department of Transport at the set rate for boarding transport workmen. I had a talk with the men, explaining our situation with the crated furniture. They would have to sit on boxes, not chairs, and there were no fancy dishes, but I told them I would endeavour to provide them with meals. They were agreeable, and even though the per diem barely covered our costs, the following weeks turned out to be some of the most enjoyable spent on the island.

One of the Shell Oil fellows fitted into our family like one of us, flinging repartee with abandon during dinner when we all enjoyed a wide range of topics for discussion. The other chap was a French Canadian who had taken this job specifically to learn conversational English. He wore a bewildered look as the puns and idioms flew. When he pulled his worn dictionary from his pocket we took time out for explanations. The senior relief continued to join us for Sunday dinners and often for coffee other days, adding spice to the life.

We had some good times with those workers and I was glad to welcome them, but looking back I see that my time and work were free to the government. By not being paid as an employee, I did not contribute to Canada Pension either. Years later, when the wives were recognized and paid for doing relief work, contributions were made and when we retired I ended up with the princely Canada Pension of $35 a month! At the time I just thought it was my duty to support my husband in his position.

Any special day, such as birthdays, Halloween, Valentine's Day, St. Patrick's Day, etc., was a time for great preparation and a distinctive theme party. On Halloween the children competed for best costume, told ghost stories and bobbed for apples in a big tub of water set up in the large old kitchen. May was Adrienne's sixth birthday so Beth and Stan decided to go all out preparing a celebration. They spent endless hours concocting a full-scale carnival to be set up near the helicopter pad. They built a wooden plane from scraps of driftwood lumber and fixed it to a pedestal. The same six children (our three—

Garry had gone to join the air force—and the relief keeper's three girls) lined up time after time for a fantasy flight into the wild blue yonder. They had even constructed a primitive typical carnival bell-ringer with wood from the beach and a ball inside to be banged up a wooden structure. The two Shell Oil fellows, the senior relief, the junior relief and Trev tried to hit the platform with a mallet to make the ball hit the bell. Surprisingly, the men often needed several tries before ringing the bell.

Beth had sent away for magic trick books and she and Stan had practised diligently during the winter months, using the family as a captive audience. Now they had become proficient enough to give a creditable performance to the assembly, Beth in her clown costume and Stan with high hat and tails. They were a hit. They dug into their bag of tricks for encore after encore. Unlike children who lived in more populated areas, these kids could not nip down to the corner store for pop, so pitchers of Freshie quenched the thirst of the active crowd. The day was sunny and warm as our family, the junior relief and his family, the two Shell Oil fellows and the senior relief milled around relaxing and socializing almost as if we were in the larger world and not on an isolated island.

Late June came and with it, at last, the tender *Douglas* to move us to our new island home. The complicated loading process of full bonnet into workboat, workboat to tender, full bonnet lifted to deck and into hold seemed almost routine now. I made my first trip in a workboat and up the side of the ship on the rope ladder. The sea was calm, and by now this feat seemed quite unremarkable after the challenges of the past eighteen months, five days, ten hours, fourteen minutes and five seconds on this first island home. As we watched Lennard Island fade from view in another magnificent sunset, we thought about the happy times and the desperate times we have lived through.

The whole experience of our first lightstation took on a dream-like quality as we sailed toward Victoria. There we would stock up on personal supplies, then change ships and head north again up the inside passage of Vancouver Island and the north mainland. Before long, we would land at Barrett Rock, at the entrance to Prince Rupert waterway. We wondered again and again what lay in store for us.

66

Barrett Rock

After leaving Lennard Island, we sailed down the west coast with balmy breezes on a rippled sea. This time the journey was short. We anchored one night off Pachena Point, and a low swell cradled us to sleep after a hectic day.

Next day we steamed into Victoria and went ashore for a few days. We visited with families, consulted with the correspondence school and stocked up on supplies for our trip north while our effects were transferred from the *Douglas* to the *Estevan*. The *Estevan* was a larger ship than the *Douglas* and was used every year to service the large buoys in the Prince Rupert Agency that could not be handled by the smaller ships out of Prince Rupert. Finally we boarded the *Estevan* and headed out of Victoria and northward to Barrett Rock, seven miles from Prince Rupert at the entrance to Prince Rupert Harbour. This time the ship turned into the sheltered waters of the Strait of Georgia, cruising the inside passage of Vancouver Island and the northern mainland, not the outside of Vancouver Island on the open Pacific with the rolling, heaving swells.

The *Estevan*, built in Scotland some fifty years before, was a steam-driven ship, so very quiet. The afterdeck had a large cleared area where deck chairs could be used. The ship glided north on rippled seas and in summer air, servicing the lightstations and buoys along the way. We looked in wonder at the vast convoluted coastline whose mountains were forested to the water as if the trees were plunging straight into the sea. There was little sign of habitation, except for the lightstations and an occasional village. Every evening, usually before dinner, we found ourselves anchored snugly in a sheltered cove.

As soon as the ship dropped the anchor, out came the deck chairs for the aft deck and we settled for a peaceful evening, visiting and watching the men throw hand-held fishing lines over the rails around the decks, intent on catching halibut. One especially determined crew member had his line over the side almost before we were securely anchored. One evening, word spread like wildfire that other crew members were playing a trick on him. They arranged to have him called for extra duties just as his line dropped over the side. As soon as he was out of sight, the line was quickly pulled up, a piece of lead pipe was tied to it, and it was lowered back into the water. The crew and passengers all gathered at the rails to watch the fun. Soon the fellow returned and languidly gave his line a short tug. Then, urgently, another harder pull. He started calling for help. "I've got one, I've got one! Oh, oh, it's a big one!" Laboriously he gathered in the handline, gradually getting the help he called for. The crews were all superb hams, simulating great effort as they helped him haul the line, all the while calling encouragement. Oh, the look of utter disbelief as he saw the lead pipe and looked sheepishly around at the grinning crowd who leaned over the rails applauding his supreme effort.

The glorious weather held. These evenings were a holiday in themselves as we sat in deck chairs in the stern, drinking in the utter scenic tranquillity and enjoying the company. It seemed to me the ship's crew was particularly sensitive to the difficulties encountered by the lightkeepers. They made the interlude aboard a ship as memorable as possible. This included the wonderful meals—too good, methinks!

One dark night, in the cabin I shared with the girls, I woke to hear a strange sound by my head. It was very loud, a sort of chomping, rustling, grinding sound. Cautiously I turned on the light and lifted my pillow. Here was Beth's pet hamster making a meal out of the sheet! It made for a little explaining to the purser. Trev secured the hungry animal in his metal wastepaper basket for the remainder of the journey.

Every day of the ten days it took to reach Prince Rupert, we were reminded in some way what to expect. Had we plenty of plastic? Did we remember to bring our umbrellas? Did we have our rubber boots? Or duck feet? The weather seemed to give lie to these dire warnings as, to our wonder, we steamed past Barrett Rock. We only caught a glimpse of a white, red-roofed bungalow and a light and foghorn atop a rock about a hundred yards out from the shore. As we entered Prince Rupert Harbour, a torrential deluge broke, and it accompanied us to the dock, confirming the crew's predictions. Undaunted, we donned rain gear and stepped ashore to explore the landfall of our new adventure—the nearest civilization to our next lighthouse.

Prince Rupert, a small town boasting only a few stores and a civic centre, was nestled at the foot of a mountain on Kaien Island. Only during the few years before our arrival had it been connected to the rest of the province by road. Until then the train, ships and, more recently, aircraft had provided communication with the "outside world." A pulp mill at Port Edward was one main source of employment and fishing was the other. Thus, during much of the year, a good portion of the population for the area tended to be transient.

When we returned to the dock, our ship had disappeared! At least we thought it had, until we got to the edge of the dock and peered wa-a-a-a-y down. The tide has a twenty-four-foot exchange here. We reboarded the ship somewhat precariously, down a long ladder held by the crew.

The rain, after assuring us of its bountiful presence, quit the next day. Once again we made our way back to Barrett Rock to offload our belongings. This time there was no cable stretching from shore to a rock. A crane on shore swung out over the water to lift our effects from the workboat to a platform.

The girls and I scrambled down the rope ladder and into the workboat for the short trip ashore. We struggled out of the boat onto the rocks, then up the bank and across a railroad track to the house.

The house itself was only a few years old, a well-constructed

Our home at Barrett Rock was a well-built three-bedroom bungalow with large windows. At left is an old concrete searchlight structure, fifteen feet in diameter, altered to house the winch motor.

three-bedroom bungalow with a living room, dining room and kitchen open area. A long hallway stretched to the bathroom at the far end of the house, past the three bedrooms. Large windows in all the rooms gave the place a cheerful feeling. An old gentleman with a wrinkled, timeless face greeted us at the door. He had been a relief keeper, basically a caretaker, until we arrived. Hospitably he offered us a cup of tea. Just as I was about to take a sip, he busily went to the cupboard saying that he mustn't forget to take his pills. To make small talk I asked him why he needed the pills. He informed me blithely that he had tuberculosis. Carefully I replaced my cup on the saucer while wild thoughts raced through my mind. How dare the department send me here with my children and even request that we let this man stay until the next day! Perhaps they didn't know about his condition. In any case, what was I to do? I lay awake most of the night worrying. Next morning I persuaded Trev to launch the rowboat on the loading platform and go to Port Edward, about two miles by boat, for bleach and disinfectant.

70

Beth and I spent the next few days scrubbing the entire house—ceilings, walls, fixtures, windows and floors. I watched the children like a hawk for any sign of illness. It wasn't until Adrienne came down with a sore throat and I rushed her to a doctor in Prince Rupert, seven miles by boat, that I found out we were probably in less danger from a person who had been treated than from walking down the streets of Prince Rupert. Well, at least we started out in a very clean house.

The true significance of the train tracks I had noticed as we scrambled ashore did not strike me until sometime during that first night. Trev said he scraped me down from the ceiling as the train burst around a corner through a rock cut, with its whistle blaring. This rock had prevented the sound from reaching us until the train was almost upon us. But the body accommodates. Soon we did not even hear it as it rushed by in the night. This train brought our mail, which was thrown off in a mailbag as the train sped away from Prince Rupert. If we had mail to go, we stood near the tracks with the mailbag and held it out as the train slowed and a man leaned out of a railcar to grab it.

After the initial cleaning, unpacking and night train adjustment, we had time to take stock of our new environment. Barrett Rock is also on Kaien Island, but seven miles around the other side of the mountain from Prince Rupert. During the war, the army had established gun emplacements here and up the side of the mountain behind Barrett Rock overlooking the entrance to the harbour. It was a very important location. The lightstation was a vigilant eye protecting Canada's northernmost west coast harbour, Prince Rupert, and the national train assured goods landed here were transported to the east. At that time the road from Prince Rupert to the rest of Canada had still not been built. As R.G. Large wrote in *Prince Rupert, a Gateway to Alaska and the Pacific*:

One other big asset was the construction of a gravelled highway from Prince Rupert up the Skeena valley to connect with the roads of the province. This road had been in the making for many years, until approximately twelve miles out of the city had been finished. It took a war, however, and the cooperation of the American and Canadian Governments to complete the job. It was opened in September 1944.

71

Barrett Rock is on Kaien Island, on the other side of the mountain from Prince Rupert. A train that encircled the coast of the island came through at night, and when mail came for us, crew members threw it off the train. Here Stan and Beth set out on the two-mile trek to Port Edward, a nearby company town and site of the pulp mill.

A quarter of a mile along the train tracks from our new dwelling were the original lightstation buildings, no longer in use but still intact with both living quarters and engine room, and only about five feet from the train tracks on the water side! I am mighty glad we did not go to Barrett Rock a few years earlier and have to contend with a noisy engine as well as the train just a few feet away.

The lightstation had been re-established farther along the train tracks where the army had built a big searchlight on shore and a concrete engine building tucked against the cliff bank where the engines to produce electricity for the army fort were located. Now this building was used for the engines that produced power for the lightstation. The old thick concrete searchlight structure at the water's edge, fifteen feet in diameter, was altered to house the winch motor. The wide opening facing the water had two curved steel doors, about seven feet by six feet. They were meant to slide, but did not. Trev promptly decided to remedy this and also to paint the whole affair, even though

*A quarter of a mile along the train tracks from our home were the orig-
inal lightstation buildings. The lightkeeper's home was about five feet
from the train tracks, so the sound of the train rushing by at night must
have been a real shock to the system.*

it meant removing the massive doors to do it. Because of his ingrained
sense of duty and his typical approach to a job situation, he needed to
bring order out of chaos (cleaning, painting and overhauling station
equipment) so that each station was immaculate with all equipment
working.

Once he had the winch house fixed, doors sliding as they should
and everything scraped and painted, he turned to the engine house.
This building was a mess, too. The engines evidently had leaked oil
and instead of fixing the leak, someone had thrown down sawdust and
rags to soak up the oil and left them there. It wasn't until Trev had
shovelled out the foot-deep pile of accumulated debris that we saw the
engines were up on pedestals. Soon the building was dunged out and
painted and the engines repaired so that they no longer leaked oil.

Next, he sized up the wood problem. On the loading ramp there
were lots of logs hauled, but not cut into firewood. We all pitched in
to help with the stacking as Trev put the old chain saw to work once

again and soon there were neat stacks of sawn beach logs drying by the engine house.

Meanwhile, I was sorting out the interior of the house. It was certainly clean now after our cleaning spree, and the accumulated washing from our travels was nearly finished. But one day when I started to fill another washtub, no water came from the tap. We thought the pump had ceased to work, but to our dismay we found that the cistern, which formed half of the basement, was empty! How could this be? The rain on the day of our arrival alone had been enough to fill the cistern to overflowing. Trev assumed there must be a leak in the cistern itself. He climbed into the empty cistern and searched every crevice, but all was sealed. Finally, he climbed on the roof to discover that the gutters were completely filled with leaves. No water could get to the cistern. The house sat next to a bank that was covered with deciduous trees and the falling leaves had packed the gutters. Once the troughs were cleaned, we waited confidently for the blessed torrents to arrive in this, one of the rainiest parts of the world. We waited and we waited and we waited. In fact, we waited the whole summer. The children carried water in pails a quarter of a mile from the spring near the old dwelling to provide for our basic needs. We filled buckets with salt water at the shore to use for flushing the toilet and carried them, slopping as we slipped and slid over the rocks up the bank and over the train tracks to the house.

Since our busy-beaver work was restricted due to the lack of water, we thought, why not just enjoy ourselves and explore the area? What a wonderful summer. Perfect weather. (Except that we could have used one day of rain to fill the cistern!)

The station was in the process of being decommissioned, something we did not know when Trev accepted the position. We suspect that the Prince Rupert Agency had not been told we were coming either, due to a lack of communication over the Ormsby Dixon line, as it was jokingly called. We were told it was named after the north (Prince Rupert Agency) and south (Victoria Agency) District Agents because the two agents had strong disagreements and were not exchanging information. We weren't aware of any of this until much, much later. This meant the care of the station was reduced. The engines powering the electric generators were to be run only at night so that the department would not need to deliver more fuel oil. The foghorn was already an automatic peep, barely audible, out on a rock. The only lighthouse duty, now that the station was shipshape, was to watch that the flashing light on Holland Rock, five miles south of Barrett Rock and visible at night, was operating. I could do little housework with the power off and water restricted.

We also gathered seafood. There was a lagoon in front of the station protected by a small island and rim of rocks. At low tide, this area was a mud flat, ideal for crabs. We found and resurrected a couple of traps. The traps served their purpose well and we had our fill of those delicious morsels. Trev and Stan caught fish, even sockeye salmon.

One of our favourite leisure activities was to explore the land. Beth and Stan often took backpacks and hiked into Port Edward, a couple of miles along the train track, for supplies. The mountain behind the house begged to be explored with all its hidden gun emplacements, now crumbling and overgrown with rainforest vegetation. Recently we learned more about the original army camp on that mountainside. Trev's cousin's husband had been sent there in 1939 just as the camp was being built. At first the army men lived in tents and then gradually moved into Nissen huts (domed metal huts on a thin concrete floor) as they were completed. Cyril told us that the searchlight building Trev had rejuvenated had been a searchlight only to spot boats arriving at the shore, not out to sea. The engine house that supplied electricity for the army fort was the same one we now used as an engine room for the lightstation. A primitive road curved up the mountain to the next level where two big searchlights blazed out into the night and two six-inch guns stood at the ready pointing out to sea. A thick concrete ammunition storage bunker was dug into the mountain nearby. Still higher on the mountain the army built the Nissen huts to house 100 to 125 army artillery and army signal corpsmen. They even had a beer parlour in the mess hut. Men on latrine fatigue duty were the sewage disposal system—they carried the buckets down the mountain and dumped the contents directly into the sea at the shore! Five hundred steps up from the huts was an observation post manned by the signal corps equipped with powerful binoculars.

What a panoramic view from the top of the mountain! To the left we looked down on Port Edward, smoke belching from the tall smokestacks at the pulp mill, fish boats at the wharves and fishnets laid over sawhorses and being mended on the docks. Booms of logs were scattered around the bay, some sprouting new growth. In the distance we could see Holland Rock and below us, our speck of habitation and a small island, with a slash through the centre, protecting our lagoon. Trev had cut a lane through the trees on the island when he could not see the flashing light of Holland Rock from inside our house. It was satisfying to him to be able to make these kinds of decisions and bring the station up to his standard without interference.

There were masses of huckleberry bushes on the mountainside, their branches laden with berries, some measuring as much as a half-inch in diameter. Stan made a bargain with me. I would make as many pies as he could pick berries to fill. This arrangement kept me quite busy until one day when Stan lay on the lawn by the house cramming his studies and he heard rustling above his head on the cliff. He peered up through the leaves of the overhanging trees to be greeted by the return stare of a black bear. Stan suddenly lost his appetite for huckleberry pie.

The office staff in Prince Rupert had told Trev that the first opening for a better position would be his. In the meantime, if he was interested, they would really appreciate it if he would go as relief when needed. It was difficult to get relief keepers in the north. Since there was nothing more to do at Barrett Rock, he said he would go temporarily where needed. One day they phoned (it was strange to us to have a phone in the house again!) to say that he would be picked up for a relief job for a couple of weeks by the *Katherine B*, a fifty-foot wooden cabin cruiser, possibly 1940s vintage. It was used by the Department of Transport for short trips to the lightstations, mostly transporting personnel, as its speed was only 8 knots and thus trips were limited to one day. It was a fairly good sea boat but tended to have a violent up-and-down action in heavy seas. We waited on the platform listening and peering into the dense fog for sound and sight of the transport boat for Trev. Suddenly there was a crunch followed by loud oaths. (Sounds carry very well in the fog.) More roaring of

Adrienne gathers huckleberries on the mountainside behind our home at Barrett Rock, summer 1963. There were masses of berry bushes there, and we brought home buckets of huckleberries half an inch in diameter.

engines, followed by loud curses and the grinding of metal on rock. Stan launched the rowboat, followed the sounds to a wayward fish-boat, then led it near our ramp where it could be beached. The boat had been badly punctured when it hit the rocks surrounding our lagoon. The crew had missed the Barrett Rock foghorn that warned mariners away from this dangerous area. At the same time the *Katherine B* arrived for Trev and, as he stepped aboard to sail off into the mist, he turned to me and said, "Take care of it," meaning the disabled fish boat. It turned out that the fisherman was very drunk. On Trev's instructions, I went to the house and phoned the fish company to come and rescue their boat and fisherman.

Stan was now sixteen and although he worked diligently at his school courses, we knew he desperately wanted to be with his peers. We realized that he would not spend the rest of his life on a lightstation, and we felt that education was very important to help him make his way in the "outside" world. I phoned the Dean of the Anglican Church asking if there was a place to board our son so that he could attend school in Prince Rupert. He told me about a boys' residence where Stan could stay for ninety dollars a month. Later I learned that all but three of the thirty boys at the residence were Indian lads from the surrounding areas. They were there voluntarily as they and their parents wanted them to attend high school. All the boys attended the local high school and were free to come and go as they wished. The government assisted the Native boys financially by paying for the residence, extra clothes, spending money and transportation home on weekends and holidays. This was only right, but I felt some unfairness that the federal government did not assist other students in similar isolated circumstances, especially their own employees. This was not a residential school, simply a safe supervised residence. There were two other Caucasian lads the first year, one from the Queen Charlotte Islands and the other from Trutch Island, a BC Telephone outpost not far from McInnis Island. The second year Stan and another boy were the only white residents.

Well, ninety dollars was half of our monthly take-home pay. We would have to tighten our belts even further. We talked to Stan about it, saying that we could scrape up the board money, but that we would not be able to afford extra clothes and spending money. If he still wanted to go under those conditions, we were willing. I told him that if it was the right decision, money would come from somewhere. He really wanted to go, so we got his things together and he boarded the train for Prince Rupert. My mind was numb.

Stan told me that the big four-storey building (including basement) was near the centre of town. It was run by the United Church with Mr. Ernie Hill as administrator taking care of the logistics and supervising the daily operation of the place. He lived with his family in a dwelling attached to one side of the boys' residence. On the main floor of the big residence were a large living room, billiard room, kitchen and dining area. In the basement was the laundry room with ironing boards. The boys were expected to do their own ironing. Five boys were chosen weekly, in rotation, to clear the tables, do the dishes and set the table for the next meal. As Stan remembers, the meals were good and plentiful. The boys were sent off to school with brown bag lunches.

From the dining area Stan could look out onto a basketball court. He started playing there in his free time and in grade twelve got proficient enough to make the high school basketball team. He became an avid player for the Rainmakers. This activity was important to Stan, not only for the game itself, but for the travel to other high schools in the province and Alaska. The students were happy that year when they won their zone and went to the provincial playoffs.

Bedrooms for the boys were on the two top floors. Stan's bedroom was at the very top—small and sparse, about eight feet by ten feet with a single bed, dresser, desk and closet. Stan also has warm memories of one young minister as a solid father figure.

There was a ten o'clock curfew and sometimes when basketball or diving practice ran late, Stan or others returned to the residence and found the door locked. They soon discovered where the all-night heated laundromats were located. Stan had other friends in town who would have welcomed him for the night, but he didn't want to impose on them. All in all, the experience of companionship, independence and responsibility outweighed the expense and the discomfort of being away from home.

Little did I know my guardian angel was sitting on my shoulder. Prince Rupert was still partly a frontier town in those days, with transient loggers and fishermen sometimes quite rough and ribald. There was not much for teenagers to do except cruise around town in a car, sometimes drinking. Stan did not have money for these extracurricular activities. He went to the Civic Centre and got himself a job, not for money but for free access to the programs. He spent all his free time there and ended up on the Prince Rupert dive team. When he joined the basketball team his time became fully occupied.

We had told Stan that he was to take the university entrance program. Not that we necessarily expected him to go to university, but we wanted him to prepare for that opportunity in case he decided to go that route. As it happened, the counsellors tried to persuade him to take the general program. To this day I don't know why, as his marks on correspondence courses were excellent. But we had given him absolutely strict instructions on that score, so he just kept repeating, "My parents told me I have to take university entrance."

Later, for Stan's graduation, we went to Prince Rupert and took several of his friends to dinner. Every last one of them had taken the easier route of the general program and were regretting the decision. One wanted to go on to become a pilot, but he would first have to pick up the extra math. And so it went with all of them. Eventually Stan did choose to go to university and become an elementary school-teacher, his first career.

While Stan was away at the school and Trev was out on relief duty, it was up to me to start the diesel engine which provided light for the evening. There were no batteries, so I had to try to crank the flywheel. No way could I build up enough momentum to go over the top. Finally Beth, who was a tiny four-and-a-half-foot, seventy-pound person, climbed on the engine and stepped on the handle as I brought it near the top. That way I could keep the wheel going faster and faster until eventually the engine started. We had power!

Trev returned from his stint of relieving. The rains came and our cistern filled. Life was settling into a routine. Then the phone rang. We were being transferred to McInnis Island. Once again, crating and packing were the order of the day. It didn't seem to get any easier with practice.

McInnis Island

On the day the tender for the northern agency, the *Alexander Mackenzie*, hove into sight, we embarked on the familiar routine. The workboat ferried our belongings to the ship and we followed. This time the voyage was only two days long, cruising the inside passage south until we came to McInnis Island at the entrance to Milbanke Sound, midway between the northern tip of Vancouver Island and Prince Rupert, with nothing between it and Japan but the Pacific Ocean. Another landfall lightstation, McInnis was established in 1921 to mark the entrance to inland waters along both north and south routes to major ports.

The swells of the open ocean are constant and huge at this island. This is where I learned the method of getting out of the workboat and onto the solid rocky shore. I was told to stand up on the bow of the workboat, which was wrapped in layers of rope to protect it from the rocks. When the boat was carried to the rocks on the crest of an incoming swell, the boat operator gunned the motor to hold the vessel there for a few moments. That's when the crew would yell "Jump!" and I was to leap immediately onto the rocks. If I jumped at the wrong

Captain Norman McKay (in the white shirt), his first mate and the crew of the northern tender Alexander Mackenzie *took us to our new post at McInnis Island in October 1963.*

moment, I would be crushed as the boat roared in again on the top of another massive wall of water after being sucked out to sea. I paid attention all right. The knowledge that I could be crushed focussed my attention sharply on learning the technique of getting out of that workboat with exact timing. I did it then and have done it since, many times. I do not remember doing it a single time.

Whoops. I thought Lennard Island was tiny. Oh my. This island was just the tip of a mountain jutting up from the sea, with a hollow in the centre into which were squeezed three houses. The lighthouse, engine room and radio shack were on a higher spot on the southwest side. Across the island from the lighthouse building, the helicopter pad was built on the highest place on the whole island. A wooden ramp from the helicopter pad ran down to the loading platform and winch house. From there another ramp led down again to the three houses, nestled in the hollow where they were protected from savage winds. Ramps were necessary between the buildings because the ground was so spongy.

We could still hear the constant roar of the swells crashing on the rocks as we scrambled over them to find the boardwalk and stroll, looking curiously all around, past the first dwelling, a small one-storey bungalow used by the other junior keeper, his wife and teenage son. We continued walking and looking as we passed the dwelling of the senior keeper and his wife. We finally reached the third house, the one that would be our new home. From the outside the suburban look of the house brought comfort. It was a solid white two-storey building. With mounting anticipation, we hurried up the back stairs and through a fairly large porch into a modern kitchen with a propane stove, no less. The first thing that caught my eye was the ubiquitous pump handle on the hall wall next to the bathroom adjoining the kitchen! On the other side of the bathroom at the far end of the short hall was a bedroom that we turned into a dining room. The living room had large, bright windows, but part of the room was taken up by stairs to the upper floor. The master bedroom was at the foot of the stairs out of the living room. Upstairs the girls chose one large bedroom and we kept the other for Stan's time home from school.

From the hall a door opened to a flight of steep stairs to the basement. Again, the basement was half cistern. The rest was chopped into smaller walled areas, one for extra groceries, another for wood and coal, and one for the wood and coal furnace. The house was quite comfortable and felt cozy.

The grounds immediately around the houses were very attractive well-tended lawns edged by flowerbeds of dahlias, carnations and other flowers in bloom. We later planted nasturtium borders to brighten it up even more.

In contrast to the manicured look around the houses, most of the island was covered in dense groves of tall, majestic firs, tangled salal undergrowth and craggy rocks. The highest point of land on McInnis had been clearcut for the helicopter pad, and massive fallen trees lay sprawled like huge pickup sticks in the surrounding ravine. What a waste!

Oddly enough, a primitive swimming pool had been built near the tower. A natural hollow in the rocks had a two-foot-high concrete wall added to two sides to deepen it and it made a splendid pool. The kids spent many summer leisure hours sunning and swimming at the pool.

We looked out our kitchen window at the wooden ramp that went up a small hill to the lighthouse building. This flat-roofed square concrete structure housed the light, engine room and radio beacon room. It was built on the southwest seaward side of the island at the edge of a cliff, seventy feet above sea level. The light itself was mounted in a lamp room atop the engine room's flat roof. It was a twin lens beacon considerably smaller than the older landfall lights. Although it was smaller, the mechanics were similar to the older type of light with a table for the lenses floating on a mercury bath. However, there was no weight to wind and no clockwork gears—the lenses were rotated by an electric motor.

The engine room equipment was similar to that of other stations except that the generators produced 7.5 kilowatts (versus 5 kilowatts at Lennard), and the coding for the foghorn was electric rather than mechanical. By the seaward wall of the engine room was a sturdy, well-varnished, immaculate "work" bench. Heaven help anyone who dared to scratch or spill a drop of oil on it. All the engines and machinery with painted copper tubing, or anything else that would take a polish, had the paint removed so that the junior keepers could polish it daily and keep it gleaming brightly, day and night. Most of the engine room walls, engine beds and floor were painted grey. The senior keeper insisted that shoes be removed before entering the engine room sanctuary and that the men wear little woollen slippers (knitted by his wife) while in the engine room! Also in this area were twenty-gallon fuel tanks for each engine. Fuel was pumped daily from the bulk storage tanks outside and the amount logged. Fog engine time was also logged and these monthly reports were sent to Prince Rupert.

A radio beacon room and office were separated from the engine room in the same building. There were two sequential beacons, one as backup when servicing or repair was needed. They were of ancient vintage at McInnis with many tubes, resistors and capacitors requiring storage in a large metal cabinet, much like a filing cabinet six feet tall and two feet square. The beacon signal was one of many at different

A former lightkeeper at McInnis Island had fashioned a swimming pool near the tower by erecting a two-foot retaining wall along the edges of a natural hollow in the rocks. By the time this picture was taken, the wall had been tossed into the woods by a typically fierce west coast storm.

locations in the northwest operating on the same frequency (300 kilocycles) one after another in a designated sequence.

Exact timing was a critical part of the beacon's function. An error of only three seconds either way was allowable, otherwise one transmission would occur on top of another and interfere with the whole system. To calibrate the beacon's clock so it would be synchronized with all the other beacons, a radio receiver and tuner, housed in a cabinet between beacons, received world time signals such as WWV in Washington, DC, WWVH in Hawaii or CBC in Ottawa—whatever signal was received most clearly.

The advantage of beacons was their continuous transmission and identical frequencies. Previously, to establish a ship's position, personnel would locate a local range station signal to establish a bearing and then change frequencies to receive another station's signal to establish two cross bearings. With the sequential beacons it was faster and less complicated to do the same thing. To have this navigational aid at a landfall lightstation was important for aircraft, and for ships arriving from across the Pacific Ocean intending to use the inside passages to north and south west coast ports.

Repairs to this equipment seemed to be constant. There were eight power tubes that had a fairly short life span, and sometimes when one burned out there would be a chain reaction to other circuitry. Trev became very adept with the soldering iron. This is one area where the knowledge gained from his service career was very useful.

Trev had been told at the office in Prince Rupert that he would need to learn about synoptic weather and that the senior keeper at McInnis Island would give him instruction. The instruction consisted of handing Trev a couple of large books. When the three keepers and their families gathered at different houses for coffee occasionally, I listened to the talk about synoptic weather and I got the impression it was very complicated. One night, in spite of my pile of work, curiosity got the better of me. Trev said, "Come on up to the radio shack and I'll show you."

Really, all one had to know were the types of clouds, as clouds have distinctive forms at different heights. Identify the cloud and you have the approximate height of the ceiling. Then you estimate the percentage of cloud cover and transpose all the information into code, with assigned numbers for each type of cloud, height of cloud and percentage of sky cover. Rainfall was collected in a cylinder a couple of inches in diameter and about a foot high. Once a day this was poured into a measuring cup, recorded, then coded. If it snowed, the snow was measured with a graduated stick at a specified location, out of the wind. A foot-and-a-half-square wooden slatted box on legs contained wet and dry bulb thermometers. The dry bulb thermometer gave the outside actual temperature and the wet bulb thermometer the dew point temperature. The difference between the two temperatures was used to calculate possible fog conditions.

All this information was coded for transmission by radio to the mainland marine radio stations. A little long division was required. We later learned that the senior keeper had only a grade four education, so he was quite astute to be able to transpose the information. The marine radio stations then broadcast the synoptic and local marine weather to all mariners: fish boats, foreign ships, Canadian registered ships and private vessels, as well as aircraft, so that they could

Inside a flat, square concrete structure on McInnis, pictured here in 1963, were the light, engine and radio room. Hanging on the wall at left is an anemograph, an instrument which measures and records the speed of wind.

prepare for or avoid local fog areas, extreme wind funnels, icing conditions and very rough sea states.

Usually the senior keeper was the one to handle the winch and apparatus to offload the supplies from the workboat. One day a few weeks after our arrival, the keeper had to make the decision whether to give the synoptic weather or land the supplies. He turned the offloading job over to Trev. It was the first time Trev had used that particular equipment and, although it was similar to the setup at Lennard Island, each piece of machinery has its own idiosyncrasies. So Trev brought the bonnet sling up slowly and with trepidation from the workboat six hundred feet below. He said he felt relief as the load neared the landing ramp—until he saw a head poke up between the ropes and he nearly had heart failure. It was the radio technician. The crew had decided the swells were too hefty to land a person on the rocks, so he chose to make the visit via bonnet sling!

Another new lightkeeping duty, begun in 1954 at McInnis, was taking a water sample and the water temperature every day an hour

A big piece of McInnis was clearcut to accommodate the helicopter pad, and the trees were left where they fell. This photograph, taken in 1963, gives a good view of the long system of ramps running to the loading platform, winch house and dwellings. The ramps were necessary because the ground was so spongy. Below, Adrienne stands on the chopper pad, looking out over our home and the light tower.

before high tide. This meant scrambling down over the slippery rocks in all kinds of weather, carrying a ten-foot pole that had a built-in thermometer at one end plus a clip to attach a small glass bottle containing the water sample. The box of samples and record of the temperatures was sent out on the tender to be forwarded to the Pacific Oceanographic Group then located in Nanaimo. They were studying long-term changes in ocean patterns that might affect fish migration, herring spawning and weather such as El Niño. The scientists of today are reaping the benefits of long-term tracking begun by their foresighted colleagues in 1921 at Race Rocks lightstation.

The duties of the lightstation in themselves were not a problem for Trev, but once again he had trouble with the senior keeper. Every six weeks to two months, when the tender disappeared from view after bringing our personal supplies, the senior keeper, with his box of liquor, disappeared for several days. This was not the only problem. Once when the population of McInnis Island gathered at the senior keeper's house for morning coffee, Adrienne, who had been playing outside, took off her muddy boots before entering their house and carefully left them outside on the back steps. That evening at change of shift, Trev was advised by the senior keeper that it was his responsibility to clean off the mud Adrienne had left on his back steps.

To relieve the tension, we decided to have a private bit of fun. We made a McInnis Crest. The top part had a tender lying off the island and a stick man carrying a suitcase running across the wavetops to the ship, to represent our desire to leave even if we had to walk on water. The middle part had two sea lions with microphones broadcasting synoptic weather and the bottom had a bucket with mops, brooms, soap and polish. Beth was taking Latin so we figured the motto in Latin as "We came, We saw, We left!" (Veni, Vidi, Exitum.)

Trev's raise in pay from a class three senior at Barrett Rock ($3,560 annually) to a junior class six at McInnis Island ($4,530) helped us to ease slightly the financial burden of boarding Stan while he attended school in Prince Rupert, but we stretched every cent we could get. A stipend of $30 a month that the provincial government provided any child (not just lighthouse children) to board while attending school away from home had helped considerably for the short time we were at Barrett Rock. As soon as I notified the school district that we were transferred to McInnis Island, we were cut off because McInnis Island was in a different school district. Because it took three to four months to answer a letter (incoming and outgoing mail happened at the same moment), it wasn't until the following year on our holidays that I was able to go to the legislative buildings in Victoria. There I discovered that McInnis Island was in one of the two still unorganized school districts in BC. The line on the chart went a couple of miles south of McInnis Island—on the water! We were told our only solution was to transfer to an organized school district or get the district organized. My effort did bear fruit eventually—an order-in-council made the last two school districts organized—but it was too late for our benefit.

The lack of help and interest from the Department of Transport in educating lighthouse children (their only assistance was to inform us that correspondence courses were available) was in such contrast to how the air force had handled the issue. Schools were provided as well as teachers and equipment, even on remote radar sites.

Once we were settled, the mountain of correspondence courses had to be faced and my thoughts turned to the stack of grade one papers for Adrienne. Here was a child who could not read or write, and it was all up to me. I felt panicky knowing I was not a teacher. I thought: I can't do this, but there is no one else! What to do, what to do? I finally decided that we would do one day's work only, not turning one page until it was finished. What do you know—at the end of the year, this child could read and write! Incredible! Satisfying.

Adrienne had always been affectionately called Pud or Puddy by the family, since the baby days when we said she was just a little pudding. One day this solemn little blonde pigtailed lady approached us and requested, "Now that I am in grade one I would prefer to be called by my real name, Adrienne." What else could we do? However, sometimes to this day, Beth will slip and call her Puddy.

Beth, now thirteen, was maturing physically and mentally and stretched her creative proclivity by "publishing" a local weekly newspaper. The editions included short, everyday news, such as the helicopter's unexpected visits, the latest hamster adventure, completion of two jigsaw puzzles, sighting of several fish boats, mowing the lawn, planting vegetables, a slide show party, a Valentine's Day party (with a detailed list of food provided), Liz (Beth), the magicians' show, comings and goings of the island's human inhabitants to and from civilization (mainly for health reasons). She also included a poetry section, weather, advertisements and some sketches to complete the weekly edition.

"It is rumoured that Miss, uh, Mrs. Hammerstein [the hamster] is expecting children around May 2nd," read one entry. Another time the weather report of the sun peeping through had an error. On the front page under weather, "should be the sun WAS peeping through." A Bulletin, "It's raining again," was followed by a Special Bulletin, "Please disregard WEATHER as it is so changeable I cannot keep up with it. Editor."

In the March 8, 1964 edition she wrote under "News of the Day": "The helicopter came bringing Mr. Sims and Mr. Morane who are installing pumps (electric)" and, under Advertisement, "One hand pump for sale. Winkle." She faithfully hand-printed two copies every week for fourteen weeks, in each edition inviting submissions of stories, poems and advertisements for publication. (She received only three entries.) One of her final advertisements threatened, "I regret that if nobody sends in any articles, this paper may have to be discontinued." There was still no interest from the community, so she stopped the presses after three months as a devoted publisher and filled more of her time writing to her pen pals.

Beth found her grade eight school work a breeze, so she had lots of free time to improvise amusement for herself. She spent a lot of time at a tiny log cabin, built by some former resident, along a trail some distance from the houses. There she concocted many elaborate skits and played all the individual parts. When Adrienne had finished her schooling for the day, she would join Beth for adventures at the cabin, or they would skip among the trees and sing together loudly and joyously, mostly songs from the "Sound of Music," one of the few records we had brought with us. There was no radio reception at McInnis during the day and often not at night either. Sometimes the girls went to the radio room at night to listen to the better radio reception there. I understand that is where they first heard The Beatles.

One of the many daily lightkeeping tasks was to record the water temperature and take a water sample an hour before high tide. The data were collected to analyze long-term changes in the ocean that could affect the life cycles of fish. Trev built this sturdy ramp to the water's edge to make the job safer for him and future lightkeepers.

The girls also had the hamsters, Hammy and Peewee (a white male), and spent hours making toys for their pampered pets. Trev built the hamsters a large cage with a ferris wheel.

As far as we were concerned, one of the greatest boons to the lightstations was the travelling library. We could send in our eclectic list and the tender periodically brought a big stout wooden crate packed to the brim with books. Beth especially dove right in and devoured the lot. Stan had the same sort of appetite for books when he was home.

It was a blessing to have all these assorted books as the winter storms swept in with a vengeance. We heard the roar of the ocean always, and when we walked outside we even felt the ground tremble when the waves crashed against the rocks. The engine room was seventy feet above sea level and some reefs stood between it and the open ocean. Yet green water inundated the building and smashed the concrete

Adrienne and Beth spent many happy days in this tiny log cabin, built by a former resident and located on a secluded trail some distance from the house. It was a great playhouse.

wall around the swimming pool, hurling parts of the wall several feet into the bush. Often sea spray blew across the island like salty bits of fluff even on a bright sunny day.

There was no way anyone could leave the station by boat with such wild sea conditions, so we were thankful for the helicopter when Trev became very ill in March and had to be flown to Bella Bella Hospital. For four days he was treated for a kidney infection before being flown back to McInnis, still sick but with medication.

Regular supply trips were made every six weeks to two months, but they were uncertain due to the sudden violent changes in weather. We still did not have a fridge, nor was there a freezer at this station. On the ship our orders were divided into "freezer" (for freezable perishables like meat), "cooler" (for vegetables) and "hold" (for canned goods and staples). The supplies for a lightstation to be serviced were collected on deck a little ahead of arrival at the station. On one supply trip the orders were brought out on deck as usual, but an emergency came up which the ship had to attend and it was many days

A junior keeper and his family climb down the rocky shore to board a workboat at McInnis Island, 1963. McInnis is where I learned how to get ashore from a workboat during heavy seas—stand up in the boat and, when the crew yells "Jump!", leap out onto the rocks.

before they could return to offload the goods. The freezer supplies had been put in the cooler and the perishables in the freezer. When they finally arrived at McInnis, the meat was high and the rest unusable. It was another six weeks before a replacement supply trip came to the island. I had developed an emergency supply of regular staples: flour, sugar, potatoes, canned vegetables and a case of bully beef on the shelf, the only canned meat I had stored. During those weeks I baked it as meat loaf, rolled it in biscuit dough, fried it and made it into stew. To this day the gang shudder at the suggestion of bully beef!

I didn't have much time to socialize with the neighbours, the senior keeper and his wife and the other junior keeper and his wife, but we did go to each other's houses occasionally for morning coffee or evening social events. The senior keeper's wife was a kind lady who catered to her husband's tastes. Our children were fascinated with sandwiches made from raisin bread because that was the only kind he would eat. The other couple were pleasant, but before I had time to get to know them, they left before Christmas when promoted to a southern station. The new junior keeper arrived before the holiday

*My garden at McInnis Island, shown here in 1963, was a success—
even in muskeg soil. Peas, lettuce, tomatoes, potatoes and green
onions flourished.*

season. He was a man alone, no family. The girls' first impression was
that he dyed his hair very black and his creased face belied the dark
hair.

Christmas was upon us before we knew it. Stan came home for
the holidays on the same trip that brought Santa, the District
Manager, and our mail and supplies. This holiday time seemed special,
our family happily together, the neighbours friendly, and we
exchanged visits. The most memorable was when we and the senior
keeper and his wife were invited to the new junior keeper's place for a
Chinese dinner one evening during the holiday. The dinner was good
and everyone enjoyed themselves until the wine began flowing like a
river. The two other keepers drank straight from the bottles, with pre-
dictable effects. Trev and I barely had time to herd our family out of
there before it got embarrassing.

The storms raged on into the new year, so Stan had an extra-long
stay at home—until February thirteenth, much to the consternation
of the school staff, who sent messages asking why he had not returned
to Prince Rupert.

95

Soon spring was poking its head around the clouds. The prospects for a garden didn't seem promising, but I sent away for seeds and a bag of fertilizer. Trev dug a patch on the hill behind our house. We were told not much would grow in this muskeg soil, but I threw fertilizer around as if I knew what I was doing, planted seeds and waited. By golly, success. Even the dwarf peas grew full-sized!

By this time Adrienne was six. When she was about two, she had fallen and damaged one of her front baby teeth. We now noticed that it was not loosening as a six-year-old's tooth should, but was solid in her gum. When we looked inside her mouth, we could see the new tooth coming through into her palate. I would have to take her to the dentist in Prince Rupert by department transportation. It was an involved procedure to make arrangements. Trev sent a radio message to the office in Prince Rupert requesting transportation for Adrienne and me. The office determined whether a boat or helicopter was available and sent a return message with date and time for transport. Weather and equipment serviceability could delay or cancel our plans. A couple of days later the helicopter picked us up and flew us to Prince Rupert. It was to be an overnight jaunt.

We immediately went to the dentist and he pulled the tooth. Then we went to the Prince Rupert Hotel and got a room for the night. I did not know anyone in Prince Rupert and the department did not get in touch with me except to notify me the next morning that the helicopter had broken down and they would have to wait for parts. They did not know how long the repair would take.

What to do, what to do? We did not have any money. But we did have education policies for the children which we bought when they were born. We were still paying monthly premiums, but it had become evident that these policies would not serve the intended purpose. So I went to the Bank of Montreal manager and he suggested cashing in the policies. I agreed and he put the process in motion.

Next I had to find reasonably priced accommodation while we waited for the helicopter to be repaired. We were walking along the street when I met one of the deckhands from the *Mackenzie*. We chatted for a few minutes and I told him of my problem finding a place to stay while we waited for the chopper repairs. He mentioned the Green

Rooms, a rooming house where casual employees sometimes stayed. Adrienne and I wandered around until we found it.

We entered the big old green building and a man behind the counter informed me that rooms were fifteen dollars a week. I could just afford this and have a little left for food. I had no choice, so I paid him fifteen dollars in advance. He led me up some narrow dark stairs to the second floor and showed me a tiny room with a thin-mattressed double bed pushed against one wall. There was a small table under a narrow window beside the bed and a dresser, chipped paint and all, about two feet away on the other wall. The bathroom was midway down a dark hall past several other rooms. I was very nervous. Later it became evident the rooms were let to transient males, but I didn't know that then.

Days turned into weeks as we waited for word to return home. I regularly phoned the department office, only to get the same reply— not today. Adrienne and I wandered the streets, going into stores just to talk to someone. It was so strange not to know a soul and to feel so alone, with no family. Even Stan was away—he had gone to the Queen Charlotte Islands for Easter with a friend. And the department seemed not to take any interest in our welfare.

One Monday, after I had just given the proprietor a cheque for the coming week, I phoned about the chopper and was told we would be leaving the next morning. I was so happy I naively thought others would be glad for us. I found the rooming house owner in the lobby and told him that we would be leaving the next morning. I said if he would return my cheque I would make him a new one for our one-night stay. He not only laughed at me but he talked about me to the other men sitting watching TV in the lobby.

Rage started to tingle in my toes and rise to the rest of my body. I managed to maintain my dignity as I walked straight to the pay phone and called the bank manager. It was after banking hours, but he explained that he lived over the bank and if I came to the side door he would let me in to sign a stop order.

Minutes after we returned to the Green Rooms, the owner lit into me and threatened to call the police and have me charged. I was terror-stricken, but managed a soft reply that I would like to speak to the police myself and left, holding Adrienne firmly. I phoned the department to confirm our departure time for the morning and was told there was more trouble and the helicopter would not be leaving the next day. Oh, God. I couldn't stay in that place another minute. Even though we could ill afford it, I phoned the Prince Rupert Hotel. They told me to get a taxi and come right over. By their response I sensed they already knew what had happened. I realized what a small town Prince Rupert was—news spread quickly! They were kind to Adrienne, bringing colouring books and some toys to the room.

Still shaken, I decided to go for a walk with Adrienne. We slipped into a back pew in the Anglican church where I thought I might find some solace. One of the pastors came over, sat down and said a few kind words to me. That did it. My eyes became water spouts as the tears spurted forth and I told him the story of the Green Rooms and of my worry that I had made too much ado about fifteen dollars. He said, "Mrs. Anderson, you don't know what you have done. That man has been cheating lonely casual workers for a long time, but no one has stood up to him!"

We returned to McInnis the next day. Months later, as Trev was going through the bundle of Prince Rupert papers that came with the accumulation of a couple months of mail, he saw a report that the owner of the Green Rooms had been sent to jail for having stolen property in the basement of the building.

When I got back, I hosted a turkey dinner for the other keepers and their families. A new couple had replaced the dark-haired junior keeper, and the women had been kind to Beth and Trev while we were away. To reciprocate I wanted them to share this special treat I had brought back with me. We used the bedroom-cum-dining room for this first social occasion. Our McInnis Crest, spoofing lighthouse life, hung in this room and throughout the meal, the other junior keeper sat near it and could barely keep from laughing every time he stole a look at it. The senior keeper took note and asked Trev what it said. Trev told him, "We came. We saw. We left." His reply was, "You are still here." Trev rejoined, "Well, we can always hope!"

Our days were full with everyone doing their work. Adrienne was progressing in grade one, Beth was always very conscientious about her studies and needed little help with the grade eight work, Trev had mastered the radio beacon and synoptic weather, the garden was flourishing—lots of full pods of peas, potatoes in bloom, tomatoes ripening, fresh lettuce and green onions to pick for salads—and life was almost a bowl of cherries.

Out of the blue, a message came from my sister that Garry urgently needed assistance. I knew she would never get in touch if it was not important. Trev sent a message to the department requesting transportation for me to Prince Rupert. The chopper happened to be in the area, having just passed McInnis. They turned back and picked me up in short order. From the time we got the message, it seemed as if there was a hand on my shoulder guiding me along the way. We arrived at Digby Island, where the airport for Prince Rupert is located. A plane to Vancouver was about to take off, but had an available seat for me. When I arrived in Vancouver, it was the same thing. From there I flew to Campbell River where my brother-in-law was waiting to drive me to the west coast.

Garry had really been a rolling stone after being discharged from the air force. He had ended up on the west coast of the island and had gotten in with some local youths who had too much time on their hands and not enough responsibilities. The others had families and homes in the area and Garry did not, so he was more or less considered vagrant. After I arrived and with some negotiation with the authorities, he was told to go home with me for a time. He did.

At the end of the school year Stan came home too. So there were the boys together again and our family complete for a while. The boys had a busy summer, swimming in the pool by the engine room, fishing and devising madcap escapades. Our philosophy was that we could not stop them from risk-taking at that age—they thought they were invincible—but we could lessen the risk by making schemes as safe as possible and by exercising unobtrusive supervision. So when they decided to rig a cable across the ravine not far from the back of our house, Trev made sure the cable was well-anchored and the single sheave pulley and handbar was safe before they dangled fifteen to twenty feet above the ravine, propelling themselves seventy feet from

Stan and Garry loved to go out fishing, and fresh salmon and cod were always tasty additions to our menu.

one side to the other. Beth had to have a go, too. The boys, who were sixteen and eighteen that summer, Garry six-foot-two and Stan catching up, would give her no handicap even though, at fourteen, Beth was a tiny person, less than five feet and less than a hundred pounds. The rules had not changed in all these years—if she wanted to enter into their activities, she had to compete on their level! I guess she determined that she would show them. She too propelled herself, dangling, across the ravine.

In their never-ending search for daredevil thrills, the boys found another outlet with a motorless scooter Garry had been given. The motorless aspect did not deter the boys. They would walk it to the helicopter pad, the highest point on the island, get good speed coming down the boardwalk ramp to the loading platform, and screech around the corner to the next ramp which came to our house. Soon that got too tame so they built a ramp jump at the bottom. Oh my!

Since the boys also spent a lot of time fishing, it pleased me immensely when they added fresh salmon and cod to our menus. But they were always hiking off with my sharp knives to clean the fish, and finally I accused them of losing all my knives. I was in the habit of peeling my vegetables into newspaper and burning the lot in the wood and coal furnace. One day Trev cleaned the furnace and came up with an assortment of burned blades!

Stan and Garry had other adventures while fishing with the small rowboat. One day we spotted a pod of killer whales close by them as they languidly cast their fishing lines, hoping a salmon would take the bait. We frantically yelled and gestured to point out the whales to them. Stan, who was on the oars, turned to see the dorsal fin of a bull killer whale rise out of the water within a few feet of the boat. The oars flashed and the boat seemed to skim across the top of the water to shore.

On every light station we lived at, there was always some unique feature of nature to study. Trev had volunteered to observe eagles for a man doing a master's thesis at the University of BC. For the next year, from high on the helicopter pad, we looked with binoculars directly into an eagle's nest and watched their daily activity. We observed them mating, nesting, hatching their young, guarding the nest and fishing—once grabbing a five- or six-pound salmon, gaining height slowly and with great effort, taking the fish to the nest and tearing off pieces of flesh to give to the young.

All our past problems faded as we contemplated the prospect of taking a long holiday, for the first time since our lighthouse adventures had begun three years before. We had been on McInnis a year, with the higher class pay, and finally it seemed we could afford to get away for a while. Lightkeepers were on duty seven days a week, eight hours a day on a three-man station and twelve hours a day on a two-man station, yet were only eligible for the same amount of holidays as any federal civil servant who would have weekends free. Thus a lightkeeper was working a hundred and four days more a year at a three-man station and nearly twice as much at a two-man station. To compensate marginally for this discrepancy, weekends were not counted during the leave time, and thus holiday time was extended another week. Statutory days were added to leave also, not time-and-a-half, but just straight days. Later, the weekend credit was discontinued and light-keepers received the same holiday time as all other employees, regardless of the extra time worked during the year.

For our holidays, transportation was provided to Prince Rupert. From there we were on our own. We did not have a vehicle now, but we wanted to see Trev's sister in Saskatchewan before returning via Victoria to Prince Rupert. With three children, (Stan stayed in Prince Rupert for school), public transportation was expensive. We took the train day coach to Prince George. There, at a motel, we realized eating out and hotel expenses would also be prohibitive. Trev scouted around and made a deal to rent a camper and truck for a month. It was a welcome trip for us, although Garry (age eighteen) took a long time to gradually join in with the family fun.

When we arrived in Victoria after the circle tour to Saskatchewan, we turned in the camper and truck and then arranged for supplies (imagine, actually hand-picking your own supplies—your favourite canned food brands, cuts of meat, etc.!), tried to solve the school problems, and crammed in as many face-to-face visits as possible. About the middle of November we boarded a bus for Prince Rupert. Never again! We travelled night and day, stopping only for brief restaurant breaks. Exhausting.

Green Island

When we arrived back in Prince Rupert to return to McInnis, Trev checked into the office and discovered we were being transferred to Green Island. We were not familiar with Green Island, but it was another promotion, this time to a senior keeper and a class seven at $5,130 annually. It was decided that the girls and I would stay in Prince Rupert at the Prince Rupert Hotel and Trev and Garry would return to McInnis to crate and pack our belongings. One of my requests was that he bring the potatoes from the garden that I had laboured over.

They were gone a few days, then returned to Prince Rupert on the *Alexander Mackenzie*. But we waited another five days before boarding the ship. We were told they needed an engine inspection, which was true, but they also knew they could not land us with the prevailing wind and sea conditions at Green Island. We had another hint of what was to come when Captain Norman McKay told me that his wife had lived at Green Island and had to break the ice on the water bucket in the house. I just thought this was a story from the "olden days."

At last we were aboard and on our way. It was now the end of November in the north, and winter storms had been underway in earnest for some time.

When I was a very young bride and with Trev at his first posting after he returned from overseas, I was disturbed at the grumbling that went on amongst the wives about the amount of time the men had to be away. I decided then that no matter where we were sent, I would look for something good about it. This attitude rewarded us with many unique experiences as we explored the less obvious features of each new location. Now I was getting my first glimpse of Green Island from the porthole in our cabin, through the blowing snow. I could barely detect a few dwellings and a tower, all jammed together—on—yes, there was—a rocky promontory. My heart sank at this bleak picture. I thought, this may be the place that tests my theory! And tested we were.

That first glimpse was short-lived. The seas were so heavy we had to turn and sail for Pearl Harbour, an hour northeast of Green Island, just south of Port Simpson. Each morning for the next few days we set out from safe harbour and tested the seas at Green Island. Finally on the fifth day we lay at anchor while our effects were offloaded. Trev went ashore with one of the early cargoes to help with the unloading. As our belongings were lifted from the workboat, the departing light-keeper's chattels were lowered to the workboat and brought to the ship. The lightkeeper himself was working the winch, so there was no time to show Trev the ropes. Our only information about the station, as the keeper and his family left and we came ashore, was, "There's a dog. If you don't want him, shoot him!"

We once again bounced on the sea, then frantically leaped the chasm from boat to shore. The ship faded into the distance as Trev and I and the children looked around our new home. We set up the beds and dug out some food. The house was the newer modern three-bedroom design exactly like Barrett Rock. The kitchen had a propane stove, and because we had been told this, we did bring propane for cooking. The house was cooling and I asked Trev to stoke up the furnace, but he came back from the basement and said, "There is no fuel down there!"

The wind had risen again to 50 knots after the lull during which we had been able to get ashore. Trev went out to survey the situation and found that the entire island, all of it, was covered with ice from

At low tide, access to Green Island is by way of the shell bar, at left in this photograph. But at high tide, only the area in the centre of the island is above water.

frozen sea spray. Any driftwood was inches thick with ice. (To make matters worse, our chain saw had been washed by a swell of salt water while it lay in the bonnet sling before the winch could lift it out of reach of the heaving sea.) Trev tied a rope around his middle, secured the other end of the rope around a steel bar in concrete, and carefully climbed over globs of ice to the beach. There he laboriously hand-sawed through the ice and then through the wood to gather a modicum of beach wood.

Now, with an armful of fuel, he struggled to pull himself over the irregular ice to the house. As he came upstairs to the kitchen, catching his breath, he said, "I think I can get just enough wood to keep us from freezing to death." And that was about it. I remember trying to write Christmas cards a few days later with a hot water bottle on my lap to take the numbness from my fingers.

Trev wrote to a friend:

How! Here we sit in our igloo and contemplate the dim distant past when we too used to sit around without problems like you people in the civilized world do. I checked into the office and was advised we would be moving immediately. Flo and the girls stayed in Rupert while Garry and I went by tender back to McInnis to pack. We only had two full days and I was sure going, from early morning until midnight besides doing a shift. The weather turned terrible, but we finally got loaded, most of our stuff got wet and we lost several articles in the chuck. Arrived back in Rupert and then lay tied up for nearly a week. Finally got away, it's four hours running time from Rupert, but tried for five days before we got ashore, returning each day to Pearl Harbour. They finally got us ashore and the other chap away and we were on our own.

MAN! You think you've had PROBLEMS. There wasn't a stick of fuel for either house and my chain saw was suffering from a bad case of dunkitis. So the farmer's fiddle [crosscut saw] was playing a strenuous tune for a few days.

Then came the blizzard, snow, ice and winds up to eighty knots. Such cheerful days and nights you should never see, trying to eke out our meagre fuel supply and braving the gales and ice to supplement it when we could. Then, oh joy, our sewer froze up! It was several days before it backed up enough to notice it. Then it froze so hard we tried everything we could to no avail. So we had to go across to the other house. Flo and Adrienne and Beth had to be escorted when it was really howling as the wind funnels between the houses and the tower—it must be over a hundred mph. So anyhoo, we received word the tender would be here on the 17th of December. We ordered a ton of coal and our Christmas supplies. Well, it tried on the 17th, 18th, 19th, 20th, 21st and finally made it on the 22nd with our precious coal and even more precious Christmas tree. We were able to eat Xmas dinner without our mitts and ear muffs on.

The helicopter pad is halfway down the island, but quite low, and it was rumoured the chopper would be around during the holidays so we were advised to clear off the pads. We proceeded to hack the fourteen inches of ice formed by salt spray blowing across the island. The wind sock, which was long gone except for several two or three inch shreds around a circular metal frame, stands on a bit of high ground behind the pad. The ice starts forming on the NE side of the pole and had gradually built up in an equilateral triangle to a thickness of forty inches today and is still building. Today we had a little short reprieve, the wind dropped from hurricane to gale force, a mere thirty knots, but built up again by evening. It's now at its customary sixty knots. We listen to the tugs and Alaska ferries talking and I guess this is THE spot to watch. Lucy Island, which is only sixteen miles south, has completely different weather. Winds seldom over twenty knots. Likewise, Tree Point in Alaska, twelve miles away.

The machinery was in sad shape too, four liquid cooled diesels and two gas engines. I sure had my go of crankiness. Seems I cranked more engines during the first month than a person should during a lifetime. There are no starters on the aforementioned and cold diesels leave me cold, or in most instances, hot, almost to the boiling point. Then, halfway through this episode, the winch engine backfired and won the battle for that day, dislocating my thumb and putting several gouges in the back of my hand.

In the meantime, back in the kitchen, the cook was having PROBLEMS. All the vegetables froze in the basement. There was a spud-peeling bee organized and the spuds commenced to accumulate, boiled, mashed, french fried. There were bags, buckets, pans and what have you, which were eventually cooked and deposited in the deep freeze. [I, Flo, was not about to waste all those hard-won potatoes from McInnis Island!] It has reached a point now where we are able to look back and things never look so bad from that angle. We are sure looking forward to some warmer weather tho', by George!

The buildings were huddled together on the highest part of the island about thirty feet above sea level—two houses separated by the forty-foot concrete tower, small engine room and the concrete foundation of the previous tower. The tangled remains of the defunct tower lay exposed on the knoll where it had been pushed from its foundation. During this frigid season the north and east sides of the houses were covered by frozen sea spray, twelve inches thick, clinging to the outside walls. At least the ice provided insulation from the howling winds. The tower also had a thick layer of ice attached, even on the glass of the lantern on the northeast side. This was not the

Green Island, shown here in December 1964, is fully exposed to the Portland Canal at the BC–Alaska border. Winters here are severe, with heavy snow and freezing winds that reach 80–114 knots.

navigational side, so Trev did not attempt to clear it. That would have been hopeless and dangerous anyway.

On the northeast side of the island, the side of the prevailing winter winds, there had been a boat house on a fairly level area. The land dropped sharply away from this flatter spot and a set of rails for launching the boat ran steeply to the water's edge. The day before we arrived, the wind had blown the boathouse over to lie on top of the senior keeper's private boat and outboard motor. He had left it like that, but later sent a message asking Trev to rescue the motor if possible. Trev was able to salvage the motor for him, but the boat was a write-off. The old sixteen-foot, clinker-built, open station rowboat had been stored outside the boathouse and so was undamaged. It wasn't until the following spring that Trev was able to clear away the debris of the boat house. It was not rebuilt, so the station rowboat had to weather the elements.

What looks like fluffy clouds in this photograph of Green Island is actually a beautiful but treacherous ice formation, shaped when layers of sea spray freeze on impact, building into the icy wind.

One day, when the wind had dropped to a scant 30 knots, I donned heavy clothes covered by Trev's raincoat as a wind protector, boots, scarf across my forehead over a toque and a couple of pairs of mitts and, with Adrienne (similarly dressed) and Trev, ventured outside to see the wonders of the ice formations. They varied according to the underlying ground features. All were built into the wind and at an angle. Here were scallops, there were icicles pointing out and up rather than down. Farther along were clumps like grapes. And, in one area, a huge buildup more than eight feet thick—like an iceberg. It was very difficult to walk over the ice as foot and leg slipped into the crevasses at about a 30-degree angle. Adrienne helped Nugget, the dog, by lifting his front feet over and then going to the back to lift his hind end.

Green Island was the northernmost manned lightstation in Canada, at about the same latitude as the north end of James Bay in eastern Canada where it joins Hudson's Bay, or Indian Harbour in Labrador. Dundas Island to the south protects Green Island from the

To keep from being blown away by the hurricane-force winds when this photo was taken during the winter of 1964–65, I had to huddle in the lee of the windsock mast. The sock itself has gone with the wind.

seas in Hecate Strait, but the lightstation is fully exposed to the eighty-mile-long Portland Canal to the north, which has a glacier at the head. When low-pressure Pacific systems suck interior high-pressure air through the narrow canal—which is most of the time—the result is hurricane-force winds battering Green Island. After we left, an anemograph was installed and winds of 114 knots were recorded. Inside the house, we could tell the strength of wind by the different creaks, whistles and roars of the building. The noise in the house resulting from these winds was so loud that we had to shout, and we developed a system of body language and eye messages to communicate.

At low tide, the island is about a thousand feet long and nine hundred feet wide, six times the size of a football field. At extreme high tide, the area is halved. At this latitude the tides range up to twenty-four feet, about the height of a two-storey building. Green Island was within rowing distance, two miles, of Dundas Island. We could see the southern point of Alaska nine miles away, and the tips of trees and the lighthouse tower at Lucy Island, fifteen miles southeast.

There were no trees on this mass of ice, but in spring a few patches of grass among the rocks broke the monotonous landscape. In spring we discovered, at low tide, a bar of seashells joining the main island with a small rock island. The crystal clear blue-green water lapping the pristine white beach brought memories of hot tropical—minus the hot—coasts. Later, at high tide, we saw killer whales slide across this white shell bar, now many feet below the water's surface.

When we arrived, there was no junior keeper. He had left some time previously (we assumed he quit when all the facilities in his house froze and there was no fuel) and there was no replacement. Garry was asked to fill in until the competitions for a junior keeper were held and processed. It gave us a break to have Garry with us. Among other things, he stood watch during the night. As the helicopter was down for repairs, Stan did not get home for Christmas.

A new junior keeper eventually arrived and Garry was taken to another lighthouse for a relief job. This new keeper was a widower and a pleasant man. We gratefully settled into the routine of work and schoolwork.

The girls could not go outside during the winter except on rare occasions, so as a diversion they started teaching tricks to the dog who had been left behind (we did not shoot him!)—a beautiful, gentle black spaniel named Nugget. They were so delighted to lavish attention on this dog and he thrived. It took a long, long time to teach him any tricks, though. I would hear Beth in the basement saying over and over again, "Roll. Roll." I teased her, saying, "He is just one of those dogs that can't learn." They paid no attention to me and kept at it day in and day out. Eventually, he rolled! After that he caught on quickly and learned many tricks. Later we found out he had had an ear infection, so perhaps his hearing was gone and it took longer to learn by gestures. We found out why he had been banished to a lightstation. He was the runt of a litter of a dog owned by one of the helicopter pilots and he had been pampered. Then, when left alone, he howled and kept on howling until he had company. This was not acceptable behaviour in a city!

Beth was fifteen years old now, and was confined to the house with no peers, no TV, no radio. But she had always been a great reader and now entertained herself by reading the several hundred romance novels left behind in the basement. She devoured every last one of them. I don't think she has read one since! Unfortunately there was no wonderful travelling library for Green Island.

Our life was quite settled, but I was still nervous about the high winds of winter and the massive swells and waves so rough no ship could approach. The station radio transmitter receiver was located in our basement instead of an engine room or radio shack, because when the wind blew it was impossible to get out to the other buildings. One time I tried to go out the basement door to get Trev in the engine room, ten feet away. As I stepped outside I was immediately slammed back against our house by the savage wind and pinned there, helpless, until a brief lull let me open the basement door and whip inside our house again. I tried not to think of our precarious position if there was an emergency. The pilots had assured me that they could hover to pick someone up if the wind dropped to 50 knots. That was some consolation, but I still felt isolated from help and was sleeping lightly.

The Heathkit marine radio receiver Trev had built at Lennard Island was in our kitchen and always on the AM frequency used by the lightstations. One night after we had gone to bed I heard Prince Rupert calling any lightstation to answer. Trev was in a very deep sleep and they kept on calling, so I got up, went to the basement, lifted the microphone, pressed the button and said, "Prince Rupert radio, this is Green Island, were you calling?"

They replied, "Oh yes, Green Island, we have a tidal wave warning. It is approaching your station and will be there—NOW!"

My mind conjured up an immediate image of a wall of water rushing to our shore. I pressed the button again and cried, "What do we do?"

"Get the lightkeepers up!"

Cursing under my breath, I raced upstairs calling Trev. I rushed to the girls' bedroom to rouse them, dig out all the warm clothes I could lay my hands on, and help them put on layer after layer—all the time thinking about that cold, cold, cold water rushing toward us. Trev was at the door by this time asking me what I thought were damn fool questions instead of doing something, anything! Of course, he was

The ice formations change with the features of the land on Green
Island. Getting around during the winter could be laborious. Below,
Adrienne helps our dog Nugget negotiate the rough patches.

thinking. We got together a mattress, food and blankets and helped the children and the dog up the metal ladders through a trapdoor to the top of the forty-foot concrete tower. We thought this was the sturdiest, highest and safest place on the island. We left them there. Then we told the junior keeper, who was up on shift in his house, and invited him to come with Trev and me to our house to listen for further news on the marine radio and broadcast radio.

The tidal wave had been generated by a severe earthquake in Alaska. We didn't know it at the time, but we were not in danger. The tidal wave came through Dixon Entrance which broadens in our area and then narrows again toward Prince Rupert. Prince Rupert Harbour suffered severe damage as did places south, including Port Alberni on the west coast of Vancouver Island. But we did not. Trev surveyed our island at daylight and could not see that any logs or debris were higher than usual. But believe me, if I could have gotten off that island that night I doubt I would ever have returned.

Eventually the lulls between storms grew longer and we could sometimes even get outside. The tender came with a welcome load of cut wood. The ton of coal had not lasted very long with the wind-chill of that winter!

As the ice melted, we looked around the island for new possibilities. I, the eternal optimist, decided to plant a garden in the spring. Although the soil was shallow and rocky, fertilizer had worked before and maybe such things as turnips, Russian kale and cabbage would have some success. That turned out to be true. The turnips were winners, some eight inches across and so many we gave sacks away to the pilots. Cabbages did well also and the carrots and Russian kale added variety to our diet. Even my little flower garden produced a few blooms.

The weather was getting better by the day and with it the unique spring and summer features of our island. Green Island was a rookery for seagulls, guillemots and oystercatchers. It was our first opportunity to observe the cycles of returning, mating, hatching of young and migrating in the fall. We counted more than five hundred seagull nests. Adrienne was overjoyed when the young hatched; she had fifteen hundred babies to check every day. The adult birds were not

The house at Green Island, shown here at Christmas 1964, was the modern three-bedroom design like our home at Barrett Rock, and quite comfortable. The howl of the wind was our constant companion through the winter, and we learned to gauge the wind speed by the different creaks, whistles and roars in the house.

happy to see her and would dive at her, sometimes hitting her head with a breast or deadly aimed poop. That didn't stop her. She just donned her dad's hard hat and a raincoat and cheerfully continued her inspection and petting.

This quiet, gentle and loving little girl, seven years old, amused herself without peer playmates, often without siblings and with her parents taken up with the battle for basic survival. She never came to us asking, "What can I do now?" Instead she created absorbing activities for herself.

Once, she asked if she could take two gull chicks for pets. She was a real mother hen, up at dawn to collect bullheads from the tidal pools, wheeling the chicks around in her doll buggy. Nugget, the dog, dressed in Adrienne's clothes, got a few rides too. I don't remember seeing many dolls in that buggy!

She named the chicks Squirt and Cheer. Like children after the

In the spring of 1965, we watched Green Island become transformed from an ice sculpture to a balmy little spot where crystal clear blue-green water lapped at a white sand beach. Killer whales romped in the waters nearby, and the island became a rookery for seagulls, guillemots and oystercatchers. Adrienne befriended a seagull, which became her pet.

Pied Piper, they followed her everywhere, growing and moving through all the stages of development. When they learned to fly they would swoop by outside her bedroom window at dawn, squawking for food. She would get up and capture delectable morsels for them!

One day she was so engrossed in her activities that she didn't notice the tide coming in, which it did at four feet an hour. Luckily Trev happened to be outside and noticed that she had been cut off by the rising water. He could still wade out and carry her to high ground. From then on she was much more cautious. Her unusual childhood teemed with practical lessons like this, with nature and self-directed discovery the teachers.

Adrienne was not the only one who had to relearn caution around the power of the sea. Our continual wood-gathering activities gave ample opportunity to experience the mighty strength of the

The houses, tower and engine room were huddled together on the highest part of the island, along with the remains of the previous tower—a concrete foundation and the tangled debris of the tower, still lying about where it had fallen. Trev's solution—bury it!

waves. Usually logs were thrown up on the rocks on the opposite side to where they could be cut into firewood. Trev would lasso the log with a steel cable and pull it around the island to the beach. If it was long, one end would often get caught by a projecting rock and have to be pushed free. On one of these occasions I went down to see if I could help Trev. He gave me the cable to hold while he pushed the other end of the log free. There was not much of a swell, but there was no way I could hold the log against the sea swell as the cable wrapped itself around and around the log. It was a serious reminder of the awesome power of the sea.

Despite the torturous method of acquiring logs, the piles of cut wood, saved and stacked, grew and gave us more confidence to face another winter.

Our outdoor activities increased with the warmer, less windy spring weather. Trev decided the unsightly mess from the demolished tower should be buried, the only way to get rid of it. He pecked away until it gradually disappeared, buried beneath a layer of soil. We planted grass seed on the soil over the buried treasure and it became a lovely, grassy knoll.

The open remains of the cistern beneath the old tower were turned into a sea water reservoir in case of fire, and an aquarium where we could keep fresh fish for observation and eventually eating. One time we put a twenty-pound lingcod in the cistern, but very soon we discovered that all the smaller fish had turned into lunch for the cod!

Stan made it home for Easter and then again for the summer vacation. The fisheries officer for the area anchored his boat on the northeast side of Green Island and spent many a weekend with us, having a bath and home-cooked meals. He took Stan out with him for a few days. They cruised the area and visited Port Simpson, as one of his crew was a young Indian lad from that village. The junior keeper went out on holidays for the rest of the summer and Stan was asked to relieve him, which gave him a chance to earn some money.

It was timely that Stan was home at the end of July, as Trev became very ill and was taken by helicopter to the Prince Rupert hospital, leaving me alone with the children. Stan was a very sensible seventeen-year-old, capable and hardworking. Ultimately though, the responsibility for the lightstation fell on me—without pay. (A wife was just expected to do her duty!) Trev was gone for nine days. They did not give him a definite diagnosis, but we suspected it was a recurrence of the kidney infection, aggravated by severe fatigue. He took it easier the next month and used the prescribed medicine. Gradually, he regained his strength and learned to relax a little.

The spectacular summer weather was also good medicine for all our winter stress. Calm seas usually prevailed and sunny days were frequent but not terribly hot. Trev and Beth rowed to Dundas Island and brought back many small fir trees to plant on Green Island. We had reasoned that if the trees would grow on Dundas Island, which received much the same winter conditions, they would grow on Green Island. A great tree planting took place, with appropriate ceremony. Sadly, they did not survive the next winter.

Stan and Beth had a great adventure one day when they rowed to Dundas Island and climbed the hill to a lake. Before they left, they studied the charts and tide tables. They were able to use the strong tides to assist their rowing and time them so they could include the expedition to the lake during the intertidal period.

The summer was also an interesting time to watch the life cycle of the birds on Green Island. The returning gulls paired up, mated, established their tiny bit of territory and built their nests. Some pairs built great elaborate nests, one mate usually bringing bits of bright material as offerings. Other pairs threw a few blades of grass around and, it seemed, laid their eggs carelessly. These same pairs carried this behaviour to the raising of the chicks. The great nest builders were also the cluck-cluckers, fussing around the chicks and guarding them, whereas the careless pair seemed just as unconcerned with the chicks as they were with their nests. We watched the chicks gradually exercise their wings, finally take their first flight and begin feeding themselves.

There were a few guillemot pairs nesting. These black birds, with high-pitched shrill calls, bright red feet and black bills that opened to show bright red inner lining, built their nests in hidden shallow rock crevasses. Adrienne would reach into a hole and bring forth a tiny bit of black fluff, the newly hatched chick.

Seven pairs of glossy black oystercatchers, with long bright red bills, laid their eggs out in the open in a slight depression of the broken beach shells. The chicks were precocious and full of personality. When we could watch them before the mother had a chance to "give them the word," we saw them peeping and pushing each other. But once they had received training, one warning peep from Mom and they would freeze, squatting inconspicuously to blend in with the terrain. The mother gradually led them to food on the rocks, demonstrating what and how to eat. Because the tide came in so quickly, a good many chicks were lost when they could not scramble to higher ground fast enough. In the evening the adult oystercatchers circled the island, each making a sort of cackling call as they circled again and again as if announcing their presence and signalling that this was their territory.

A raven often kept Trev company while he cut and stacked the beached logs. When he stopped to rest, the raven serenaded him with its melodious song. But when I came around, the bird was silent. I guess it finally accepted me, as one day when I was there, it broke out with beautiful music.

Adrienne's two seagulls were now flying and joining in with the other seagulls, but still returning to her for a handout or just a visit. We wondered if they would migrate with the rest, who were now leaving in small bunches, or try to remain on Green Island for the winter. In this scenario they would likely perish. We banded them and hoped. Long after the others had left, they circled the island many times and finally flew off.

September was fast approaching. Stan would be returning to Prince Rupert to finish high school, and Beth was chomping at the bit. She was now sixteen and we had promised we would try to find a suitable place for her to board if she finished her year's work. She was always conscientious, but now with the enticement of a life with peers, she concentrated even more and completed the work by the middle of August. To take a full slate of courses for a school year required a lot of tedious, time-consuming written work. It was not very challenging and often boring, more so because of the time it took for papers to be sent in and returned—anywhere from three to four months. But the children gained great self-discipline in study habits and we were very proud of them.

We contacted the Dean at the Anglican Church in Prince Rupert and he set up a place for Beth to board. It was with a family who had just lost the father and the mother needed to return to work. I was apprehensive as I could not go in myself to check it out. As Beth and Stan left for Prince Rupert after Labour Day, I found it hard to see them go.

Now, with the three oldest children gone and the thought of three months' housebound winter, I searched for ways to keep from getting bushed. I saw an article in *Chatelaine* magazine that some universities were offering courses by correspondence. I wrote to all. Most had residency requirements, but at Mount Allison in New Brunswick, it was possible to complete a degree by correspondence.

I sent my transcripts from Victoria College, now twenty years old, and was accepted. I signed up for two courses, my best and my worst, math and French. I thought if I could cope with those, I could tackle anything. As it turned out, I loved the challenge. I was surprised to find one does not really forget and that stored knowledge can be dredged up to form the basis for new work.

One day a notice in the department's news brochure caught my eye. It was from a church group in Australia wanting to write to women on lightstations in Canada. I started the wheels in motion by answering the article. Eventually a group in Melbourne took me on, a different person each time answering my letters. Gradually my correspondents were whittled down to a handful of regulars, resulting in long-lasting friendships where we shared experiences in raising children and exchanged descriptions of our different countries. These treasured letters filled a great hole in my life.

By now, the occasional blast of winter was reminding us that soon we would have to find indoor activities like university courses and pen pals. One Sunday the fisheries officer had dinner with us. His boat was anchored off the northeast side of the island, the side most vulnerable in winter storms. He was telling a story when I heard the wind rising. I mentioned the wind to him and he just said, impatiently, "Yes, yes." The ominous sounds in the house rose and I went to look out the bathroom window. Just then, we heard the awful sound of metal grinding on rock. We all raced down to the boat, but by this time the wind was howling and the sea was up. We could do nothing but watch the boat being thrown farther onto the reef with each surge. We radioed for a tug to haul the boat off the reef, but no one would attempt such a feat under those conditions, especially since no lives were in danger.

The officer stayed with us a week, and during this time this charming guest became a surly man as his boat was tossed farther and farther ashore. As it turned out, it suffered practically no damage, only a bent propeller shaft, because the rocks were rounded and rose gradually. Amazing.

When there was sufficient break in the weather for a tug to come near, Trev helped put a line from the fisheries boat to the tug and ferried him back and forth with our dinghy. At high tide the boat finally came free and we watched him and his boat and the tug fade into the distance. We never heard from him again.

The local fisheries boat, anchored off the northeast side of Green Island, runs up on a reef during an early winter storm, 1965. Conditions were so bad that no tug would venture in to haul the boat off the reef. The fisheries officer had to stay with us for a week, waiting for a break in the weather.

We happened on another unexpected indoor activity when we learned that we could receive television signals at Green Island. We ordered a black and white TV, our very first.

Trev had said no TV while we were in the air force. I think if we had stayed with the service, we would have had to get one—the children had started to go to other people's houses to watch the programs—but since then it had not been an issue as there was no reception at Miracle Beach or at the other lightstations. I believe the lack of TV helped Beth and Stan become avid readers.

But now, being so isolated, it felt good to bring in the outside world peripherally. The signal was from Terrace and we got some locally produced programs which were corny but fun. There were also several good children's programs that were ideal for Adrienne now that Beth, her playmate, was at school in Prince Rupert.

Winter storms began in earnest, but with not quite the same vigour as the previous year. There was not as much snow around the houses and the ice buildup was not as deep nor the ice shield on the houses as thick. Our days were filled with the routine of school. Adrienne's instruction came first, and when hers was finished for the day I began my university correspondence and Trev, who had enrolled in a basic radio electronics correspondence course, set to work at that. The days slipped by and soon it was Christmas, with Beth home for the holidays.

It was then we heard that the home where she was boarding had been a disaster. Even though we were paying room and board, I had expected Beth to clean up after herself and help as she would at home. However, she ended up being live-in help, cleaning house and washing dishes while the woman and her sixteen-year-old son relaxed in the living room. The boy, who had just lost his father, must have resented a stranger in his home and began physically pushing Beth around. She finally phoned Stan, who then went to the pastor, who quickly arranged another place. This new situation was much more suitable, with a girl about Beth's age and a fair but firm mother.

Stan had stayed in Prince Rupert so that he could go with the basketball team to Alaska. We had planned to blow the foghorn for him when he passed by on the Alaska ferry. But the weather did not behave—"down mainland inlet winds" were blowing their best. At times like this, the ferry hugged the mainland coast where the effect of the wind was not as fierce.

The excitement of Christmas soon dissolved and Beth was back in town at school. Our daily routine of schoolwork, baking, weather reports, engine maintenance, cleaning and fog vigilance was happily interrupted whenever the outside world found its way into our fortress of isolation.

In February 1965 there was notification of a new Canadian flag—a red maple leaf on a white background with two red bands bordering. Trev chose a good straight log snatched from the sea to shape and paint. In July we were told to take down the good old red ensign and raise the new Canadian flag. We did, even holding a bit of a ceremony as Trev sadly lowered the red ensign, which he had fought under during the war, and tucked it away.

The upcoming federal elections provided more diversion. Lightkeepers on isolated stations do not get to vote, which means we

The family raises the new Canadian flag on Green Island, July 1965. Trev was proud to fly the flag and had pulled a good straight log from the sea to use for a flagpole. But he was also sad to say goodbye to the red ensign, under which he had fought during the war.

felt—and actually *were*—disenfranchised. At Lennard Island we were fortunate because the Tofino lifeboat was authorized to make regular trips to Lennard Island and we were able to vote. But at Green, as at most stations, keepers weren't so lucky. The district manager in the northern agency must have thought the same, but decided to do something about it. He somehow got the powers-that-be to make each lightstation a polling station. The helicopter brought the paraphernalia associated with this position and we had to perform all the offices. I remember Trev got nine cents for enumerating our three names. We started following the campaign on the radio and TV.

The junior keeper often came in for coffee, and great discussions would ensue—at least between him and Trev. The incumbent in our area had been the Member for a long time and was supposed to be the best bet, but if I brought up another point of view I was shushed and told that there just was not another serious candidate. Well, I got madder and madder. I thought to myself: no one is going to tell me how to vote!

Election day came. The helicopter brought the great metal ballot box with the big padlock on the clasp. We set up our voting room with the screen that had been provided. With great ceremony we cast our individual votes. The helicopter came and captured our ballot box.

That evening we invited the junior keeper to join us to watch the results on TV, broadcast from Terrace. An announcer sat at a desk reading the results, as a hand held out a card showing the name of each polling station and results, and placed it in a device facing the screen. The card for Green Island came up showing—number of votes, three, two NDP and one (I can't even remember), whatever! So there. I believe I was the only one in the district not to vote for the incumbent.

Other than these "big" events, we had few visitors at Green Island to relieve our isolation. The occasional workman from Prince Rupert came to overhaul the diesels and stay overnight if necessary. (The lightkeeper's wife was expected to provide accommodation and meals.) Sometimes the church boat the *Crosby IV* made the trip bringing Stan and Beth if the visit was during a school break. Most of the time there were no women aboard, but once the minister's wife came ashore for a visit. I whipped a frozen roast out of the freezer, put the oven on high and managed to give them a reasonably festive dinner while we visited. We never knew ahead of time if or when visitors would arrive.

One time the church boat brought Stan and a close friend, and the return trip to Prince Rupert is one they still talk about. The boat stopped at Lucy Island, the next lightstation, fifteen miles from Green Island toward Prince Rupert. While they were ashore the farewells were prolonged and the wind rose. By the time they got underway the seas had mounted and they were taking green water over the wheelhouse. Stan said there was water spraying through the seal around the windows in the cabin. I hear tell there was a good bit of *mal de mer*!

One day two smallish sailboats neared the shore at Green Island and Trev invited the crew ashore. The people were interested in the lightstation, but they were also interesting themselves, most having some connection to UBC. Some were in education and others in architecture. I remember particularly one who had graduated in Japanese studies and would be going to Japan to work. She showed me the basics of how a word was built in Japanese printing.

Another time a forty-foot powerboat came near and a head poked out of the forward hatch, calling, "Which way to Alaska?"

Trev pointed in the direction of Alaska. The voice on the boat had sounded somewhat slurred. The boat turned and went in the opposite direction, toward Dundas Island, away from Alaska. Not long after, they were near our shore again and the head called, "Which way to Alaska?"

Trev again pointed and said, "It's still that-a-way!"

Earlier in the year, as the storms abated, a fish boat had come close to the island and the helmsman leaned out the window to wave. Next time he threw a beautiful salmon ashore. So it went, with more visiting as he passed by. One day he arrived with his wife and children and they came ashore for a visit. They were from the Native community at Port Simpson and very likable people. He told us that drinking was such a problem on the reserve and that he and his wife had once been just as involved. With the birth of their first child, they were so happy that they made a pact not to drink any more. It must have taken a great deal of strength, but they succeeded. Now he was one of the few in his community to own his own boat. He also told us that with the return of the seagulls each year, his people would come to Green Island to gather fresh eggs. Apparently, the gulls would continue to lay more if some were taken, at least for a time. This was great news for Adrienne. For a while it was Easter every day as she gathered some eggs and packed them in cardboard cartons layered with green grass, ready for our friends to pick them up. They were much appreciated by the community in Port Simpson.

One Sunday, this man and his family came ashore with his mother-in-law. She had just heard of the loss of a distant cousin on the Skeena River so they had taken her for an outing. She told us her childhood memories of the food-gathering circle route taken by the Port Simpson people. They would go to the Skeena River to catch fish and preserve them, then to Dundas Island for deer, on to Green Island for seagull eggs and finally they would winter in Port Simpson. We were fascinated hearing about this living history.

We treasured these infrequent visitors, but I found myself with less and less physical stamina to entertain them. There were other ways I noticed my energy was depleted. On the frequent sunny days I was often outside helping Trev stack wood, and I had absolutely no strength. I would lift one piece at a time and then have to rest before attempting to lift another. I finally decided I would have to see a doctor. It was just as easy to fly to Victoria to our family doctor than to try to find one in Prince Rupert.

The chopper picked me up and flew me to the airport on Digby Island, where I boarded a plane for Vancouver. I thought I had managed to avoid becoming bushed, but when the man sitting next to me began to chat with me, I noticed a strange look on his face. It was then I realized that, instead of answering him out loud, I was mentally answering his questions! I giggled to myself, thinking, you're not bushed, Flo—not much!

I spent some time in Victoria being tested for this and that, including pernicious anemia, which sounded like a death sentence! However, further testing found that my thyroid was not working. I was monitored for a week or so with prescribed medicine. Then I flew home again, where I slowly regained my energy.

With the return of my health, we were once more very interested in the department's yearly transfers and promotions. We had reached the limit of our endurance with frigid, desolate and confining winters at Green Island. On the radio we heard messages going back and forth signalling staff turnover. Trev had sent in his usual long list, requesting any equal or more favourable location, or anything higher than our present position. We had always thought it would be interesting to go to Langara Island off the northwest end of the Queen Charlottes because of the diversity of birds and other wildlife, or Ballenas Island near Parksville on Vancouver Island, which was a lower class position but was located in the south, so supplies and transportation would not be as costly. But we soon heard a message telling another contestant that he had been selected for Ballenas.

The other important event at this time was Stan's graduation from high school. We were taken to Prince Rupert for his ceremony in the department helicopter, and there we had confirmation that our struggles had all been worthwhile. Stan applied for entrance to the University of Victoria and found a job in Prince Rupert to save for his tuition and living expenses.

When we returned to Green Island the "pleased to advise" messages began to arrive—the department's signal that they were offering Trev a new position. One offer was to Race Rocks. Even though it was the same class as Green Island, its location was tempting—close to Victoria where Stan would be attending university and Beth would have access to high schools. After several days' discussion we decided to accept Race Rocks. My secret thought was, "Oh dear, another rock!"

The old pack 'em up and crate 'em began once again. At least this time it was summer, with warm weather and glassy seas. Still, the packing and crating seemed endless.

Toward the end of the packing, when we were expecting the Estevan to appear in view, we took a break to sit outside in the sun. Lazily we watched a thirty-foot cruiser putter past about a half-mile off the north side of Green Island. Trev put the binoculars on it as it seemed a strange craft. Suddenly black smoke began belching from it.

Kids and dogs and people spilled onto the topsides. We wondered how so many could fit in it. A man got in a dinghy to monkey around with an outboard engine which was attached to the stern of the cruiser. They did not head toward us, which seemed the most logical thing to do, but limped past and disappeared around the end of Dundas.

That evening the *Estevan* steamed by. It didn't stop to take us and our chattels aboard, but sailed on by and disappeared around the end of Dundas. Then it reappeared towing the crippled boat. They anchored farther along Dundas and it wasn't until we were aboard the next morning that we heard the story.

Two families had packed all their belongings, kids and dogs, and were heading "north to Alaska" in this makeshift boat—topsides hastily enlarged with crudely cut unpainted plywood. Somehow they had made it this far from Seattle! After being crowded into that small space for such an extended period, the "big city" kids raced around the decks of the *Estevan*, delighted at the freedom and the treats that the crew gave them.

We took a short detour nearer to Prince Rupert, where another boat took them in tow. Then we headed south, looking forward to our next adventure.

Race Rocks

The trip south went quickly, as the lightstations and buoys had already been serviced on the *Estevan's* yearly trip north. After a brief stop at Merry Island to drop off the couple from Lucy Island, we were soon at Race Rocks and ready to begin unloading. The sun shone brightly as the workboat pushed smoothly across the rippled sea to a crumbling stone "wharf." It was a high tide so the girls and I could just step out of the boat onto the dock and walk quickly ashore to explore our new home.

A friendly little man greeted us and called a hello to "PUD"! The look of dismay on Adrienne's face was something to behold. How could this stranger know her intimate family name which hadn't been used now for three years? The mystery was solved over tea. The small, cheerful man was the relief keeper for the southern agency. While at Lennard Island, he noticed names and height marks on the door frame in the old pantry. Since we were the only family with four children, he correctly deduced the measurements were for the Andersons. We hadn't realized that we had left a personal information trail.

As we began this new phase in our lives, it seemed different from previous stints. With more experience at handling various situations, we felt more confident. Just being nearer to civilization gave us more security. Even the house that we were moving into was familiar. It was

By the time we were posted to Race Rocks, pictured here in July 1966, we were much more confident about living on a lightstation. The building on the right is the engine house with the beacon room and the fog alarm tower. (B. Cruise photo)

the same design as the ones at Barrett Rock and Green Island, and just six months old, so setting up our belongings was a breeze. One notable difference was the full-sized basement (the cistern was located outside) and, amazingly, there was an oil furnace! No more wet driftwood to snatch from the sea, cut and stack to dry. The only bothersome part of establishing our home was the dynamited rock, sharp underfoot, still surrounding the house. It made moving in difficult, especially since no walkway had been built.

The tower was an engineering marvel. It was unique—tall, built of granite and sandstone, and painted with white and black horizontal

In this photograph of the engine room at Race Rocks, taken in about 1970, you can see the painting on the compressed air tank.

stripes. The story goes that much of the stone for the tower was brought as ballast in ships from Europe. The internal circular stone stairway, with steps made from pie-shaped sandstone slabs with circular knobs on the pointed ends, was an integral part of the stone walls. The knobs were stacked on one another to form the central newel post. Ninety-nine stone steps led to the lantern top where the main light was surrounded by parabolic mirrors, the lot sitting on a round container full of mercury.

As the mirrors had to be shielded from the sun during the day so they would not focus the sunlight and start a fire, Adrienne earned her allowance by running to the top before sunset every day and removing the curtains. In the morning she would put them back up in front of the mirrors.

Built in 1860, the stone walls of the attached dwelling were fused with the walls of the tower. This rare stone dwelling had been occupied until our new house was completed, six months before our arrival. Both the tower and house were built at the same time as Fisgard Lightstation at the entrance to Esquimalt harbour near Victoria.

The first lightkeeper at Race Rocks had not worked out, so Mr.

Davis, the lightkeeper brought from England to man Fisgard, was sent to Race Rocks and remained the lightkeeper there for almost six years.

Like Lennard Island, Race Rocks had two Fairbanks Morse kerosene engines and two Lister diesel engines powering two 5-kilowatt generators. A beautiful painted landscape adorned the side of a huge compression tank that stood upright in a corner of the forty-foot-square engine house. The delicate artistry on the tank contrasted sharply with the stark cold machinery. The horn was similar to the one at Lennard Island. When originally installed it could not be heard at sea from ground level, so an attached tower was built facing the sea and the horn raised. At forty feet it was finally audible fourteen miles away.

Race Rocks had radio beacon equipment in a separate room adjoining the engine house, as at McInnis Island. On a desk to one side of the radio beacons was a lightstation radio transmitter. In a twenty-four-hour period, seven weather reports were broadcast to Victoria Marine Radio for rebroadcast as local marine weather and forecasts for all water traffic: big ships, freighters, tankers, ferries, commercial and private fish boats, sailboats and small local boats. Included in the weather was wind speed from an anemograph, and barometric pressure.

As at McInnis Island, the radio beacons on Race Rocks were checked frequently so that the timing would not be out by more than three seconds. Race Rocks was in sequence with some American Coast Guard stations, a military outfit, and they would get very perturbed if the timing was not right.

The significance of the weather reports was expressed by a Canadian pilot boat skipper who guides three-hundred-ton foreign vessels through our inland waters. He said that the single important feature of a lightstation was all the information on the local weathers. These reports cannot be duplicated entirely by machines.

Today, the government is ploughing ahead automating the lightstations—using electronics. Electronic equipment breaks down, and with no lightkeepers to manually activate light and foghorn, there is no backup system for the computerized complex. Lightkeepers can not only quickly solve a problem, they can improvise an alternative solution.

There is no wait for a defect to be reported and no need to arrange transportation of technicians and parts (weather permitting!).

But the crisis of lightkeepers' extinction was well in the future. In 1966, we were still surveying our new environment at Race Rocks. Several smaller buildings, painted a red brick colour, were scattered around the area: a now unused chicken house; a fuel shed built on stilts used to store kerosene, gasoline and lubricating oil; a storage shed; a boat house; and a long building east of our house that had been a blacksmith's shop. In this long building, one had a sense of history. There were relics of an aged forge—now cold but waiting to be fired— and huge bellows, six feet long and three feet wide, thick with dust. As we gazed out the door of the old blacksmith shop at the massive historic tower and attached stone dwelling, we pondered the life of the self-sufficient lightkeepers in bygone years. How primitive it was—no central heating, probably not even hand pumps for water distribution, and much more isolated without radio communication.

In contrast to the stone tower and old house, today's lightkeepers' dwellings, a smaller version for the junior keeper, were a contemporary design. Red roofs on all structures blended past and present, and shining white paint applied to the houses gave vibrant visibility, which definitely aided navigational safety. The crowning touch—huge bands of black and white rising in the air with the tower's surface, and capped by a blood-coloured lantern top—transformed this inconspicuous lump of land into a prominent display of visual and aural warning signals.

Whoops! On closer inspection of this distinctive bright presentation, we saw the jagged hunks of rock and oil barrels—some empty, some full—carelessly strewn around in two-foot-high dry grass. The crumbling stone and concrete landing wharf was in very sad shape. It looked like our work was cut out for us again.

Race Rocks is located at the entrance to busy Victoria harbour and the military harbour in Esquimalt. It is a navigational hazard with the combination of treacherous waters, low land, surrounding rocks, frequent fog conditions and high winds with blowing spray. So it requires a high visibility as a vital signpost to small but dynamic Victoria harbour; big, industrious Vancouver harbour; and even ports north through the Strait of Georgia and south into Puget Sound with its bustling ports of Seattle and Tacoma.

Race Rocks is eight miles from Victoria in the Juan de Fuca Strait and is separated from Vancouver Island by Race Passage, a half-mile waterway between Race Rocks and Bentinck Island. The passage is swift flowing—up to 6 knots, like a rushing river with whirlpools and eddies. When a strong ebb tide meets a brisk west wind, the standing waves are fifteen feet high. There is a passage, navigable only by small craft, between Bentinck Island and Rocky Point DND (Department of National Defence) property and ammunition depot. Race Rocks is just that, rocks. The larger rock, on which the lightstation is built, is about four hundred feet in diameter.

We were barely organized when a message came advising us that a work crew of five men would be arriving to build the new wharf. The office "expected our usual co-operation," which meant they expected the men to be boarded and housed at our place. I had no way of getting into Victoria to shop. We could go to Pedder Bay with the station boat, but there was no bus to take me the twenty miles from there to Victoria, and we did not have a car. I made up a long list of supplies and asked Victoria Marine Radio if they would phone the order to Eaton's. It was to be delivered to Race Rocks by the department, but paid for by us in advance. The groceries came at the same time as the workmen, so I didn't have a chance to prepare anything ahead nor put the groceries away before plunging right in to feed the hungry horde.

Five big, hardworking, likable men arrived. It was a very hot August and I did not look forward to cooking day and night over a hot oil stove. Each morning I got up in time to have breakfast made for the family and five men so that the men could start work by 8:00. They came in at 10:00 for coffee and snacks and after that break there was just time enough for me to prepare lunch. These men needed substantial meals to continue the backbreaking work of rebuilding the stone and concrete wharf using wheelbarrows and a hand cement mixer. One day I watched as a particularly large man, who looked like a weightlifter and stood well over six feet, loaded a puny wheelbarrow with big rocks. The handles bent as he heaved up the load to wheel it to the wharf area.

In almost no time, the men were in the house again for afternoon coffee and as soon as they went back to work, I did too, preparing a big dinner. While the men relaxed a little after dinner, I cleaned up and fixed a few things for the next day before we had a goodnight cup of tea and some goodies. The men were a considerate bunch, pleasant to have around, but it was such a lot of work. They were with us more than five hot weeks. I don't know how I did it.

Meanwhile, our schooling routine hit some snags. I did not have the time for my own courses, with five workmen to feed and house. Nor could I arrange to board Beth so that she could attend a school in Victoria. Besides no time, there was no transportation from Pedder Bay to Victoria and no direct telephone. Our only communication was by relaying messages through Victoria Marine Radio. Beth had to continue school by correspondence. She was disconsolate, especially after having spent a year with her peers at school in Prince Rupert.

We needed time to size up the situation before allowing her to board in town. Then Trev was notified he would be going to Ottawa for a beacon course in January. We decided to take our holidays then and accompany him. Beth reacted by refusing to complete her correspondence assignments. We suggested she stay in her room until the work was completed, and it took three months before she capitulated.

Beth became more interested in life at Race Rocks when, almost as soon as the workmen had gone, KOMO TV from Seattle, contacted us to do a lighthouse Christmas program. At first we were not too keen, but they persuaded us as they talked about picturesque Race Rocks lightstation and said how appropriate it was for a Christmas program since we had a young child. We finally agreed and it turned out to be quite an enjoyable learning experience. A month before the festive season, we spent five days pretending it was Christmas. The crew concentrated on filming our Christmas preparations—baking mincemeat tarts and getting the turkey ready, wrapping elaborate fake presents and decorating the house, and setting the table with our best china and crystal for the festive Christmas dinner. They interspersed those scenes with shots of the island, wildlife and brief interviews. We had two Christmases that year!

After the film crew left, I had some free time. I went to Pedder

Bay via station boat and from there a kind friend drove me to Victoria. There I was lucky to find an old secondhand Chev sedan in splendid condition. It made our life much easier. Now I could go to town for personal grocery shopping or visiting or medical appointments. I also thought, now that we had our own transportation, we might be able to engage in some "regular" activities, weather permitting—which was always a big "if" because the westerly wind could rise quickly and churn up the sea.

Adrienne had been longing to take ballet lessons. We tried, but anything that involved a regular day every week just wasn't feasible. Her lesson was on a Saturday. Well, Friday the seas would be calm and Sunday the same, but Saturday might be blowing a gale. By going to town a day ahead of her lesson and staying overnight with my folks she did enjoy lessons for a couple months, but this arrangement was too difficult to maintain and we had to give it up. I also had a hankering to take some art lessons, but it was the same scenario. I gave up trying to take lessons and instead experimented and taught myself over the next few years. I realized a talent for seascapes, painting about forty creditable oils over the years plus some still lifes and landscapes. The kids asked me why I always painted the sea and my answer was because I liked to paint the sea! From every window at Race Rocks I could look out at the kaleidoscopic wave colours and turbulent ocean conditions. It was never the same. I watched the restless panorama and tried to capture, as inspiration struck, the different facets of that powerful moving vista with brush and oil on canvas or any handy hardboard.

My university studies had to be put aside. There were just too many visitors and workmen and other interruptions for concentrated study. But I did complete the courses I had started, even writing the exams after locating an invigilator. I was satisfied that my marks were fair, especially French, 68, and math, my favourite, 90 percent.

Too soon it was January and the bustle to get ready for our combined business and vacation trip to Ottawa. We left a very mild winter on the coast—Adrienne had even been running around in bare feet—to land in Ottawa in 20-below weather. What a shock! We had lived in Ottawa for four years at one time, but one does forget the forgettable. We were startled into remembrances with the ice and snow and Ottawa wind-chill factor.

The girls and I bought and bundled up in more appropriate clothes, then set out to explore the city while Trev attended his radio beacon course. We visited all the national sights—Parliament Buildings, art gallery, museums, shops—soaking up culture after the rural desert of the lightstations. It was interesting to reacquaint myself with the city and note the changes. Ottawa was no longer a small civil servant and military town but a bustling cosmopolitan city. The winter weather also reminded me that BC was the place to live!

Trev's course finished and we boarded a bus to Niagara Falls for a visit with my sister and her family. While we were there, my brother-in-law helped us find and buy a truck in perfect condition with low mileage and the right price. Before leaving Victoria we had set up a loan at our bank in case we found a reasonably priced truck and camper to buy. Now we looked in vain for a camper to complete the rig for our proposed trip south to warmer climes, then west across the continent and up the west coast of America to BC.

There were no campers in the east—most people used trailers—so we imported a light, simple eight-foot one from Buffalo. This combination served us well for the next seventeen years. Without the camper and truck we could not have afforded to go on holidays once a year. As lightkeepers we did not have the option of staying at home for holidays, as a relief keeper had to live in our home while we were on leave. Now we would be able to take holidays every year.

We set off for Washington, DC to visit friends and take in the highlights there. Then we headed south to Florida, explored New Orleans, spent a couple of days at Disneyland in California, and enjoyed all the state parks along the way, which were not crowded that time of year. It was a trouble-free, fun-filled and scenic trip. We headed home with restored spirits after so much chaos and crisis the last six years.

Back to the grind. Trev concentrated on the outside, moving the jagged rocks left behind by the blasting that had created a level spot for our house. The rocks were scattered far and wide, haphazardly hidden in the long grass. We piled them around the foundation of our house.

Stan helps to clear storm debris so that the station boat can be launched. Over the course of our lighthouse life we got to watch plenty of dramatic winter storms, and we can understand why people travel to the west coast of Vancouver Island just to see them.

Once the rocks were cleared and oil barrels rolled and stacked neatly, our house was more accessible. Trev turned to the grounds using a trusty scythe to hack away the dry grass so that he could push a hand lawnmower over the stubble. Cutting that large area once with a hand lawnmower was enough—we promptly invested in a power lawnmower. Not too long after this purchase the department finally sent out a power mower! But we really needed two mowers to keep the extensive grassy areas looking respectable.

Now that most of the "lawns" were in shape, on one side of the house we built stone steps leading down to a sunken garden. Protected from wind and sea spray, a patch of lawn and pockets of a rock garden planted with gloriously coloured portulaca flowers needed little water and were hardy enough to withstand the punishing elements.

The department next elected to send out hundreds of bags of soil to cover the blasted rock. The soil would have just disappeared through the crevasses in the four-foot pile of rocks, but Trev laid the empty gunny sacks over the rocks and then added a few inches of soil on top of the sacks. We planted grass seed but the constant strong wind blew the seed away almost as fast as it was planted. It took many years for us to establish a more manicured lawn area around the house.

I tried planting some fruit trees. They struggled valiantly, but the salt spray shrivelled the leaves so that they dropped off. New leaves appeared nearer to the ground, but each time sea spray again shrivelled the leaves and eventually the trees just gave up. We didn't have much luck planting trees on any of these windswept rocks. With constant wind and minimal water during the summer months, any type of garden was difficult to grow. We had some success with a narrow rose garden sheltered by some rocks, but it took a lot of effort to keep it growing.

As on other lightstations, the water supply at Race Rocks was not abundant even though there was a cistern. It was situated outside, between our dwelling and the tower, in a deep valley in the rocks. When we arrived the cistern was covered with a planked wooden top, but that was later replaced by a concrete cover because debris and seagull excrement fell through the cracks and polluted the drinking water. Rainwater for this cistern was gathered from the engine room roof, the old dwelling roof and our house roof.

The old dwelling, now that it was no longer inhabited, was still useful in many ways: as a rain catcher, as a protected entry to the tower itself and as an empty cavern to be transformed in Adrienne's imagination into a hospital, a store, a giant playhouse or sometimes a theatre. The stairs to the tower made an excellent stage entry with wonderful sound effects, strange echoes and eerie, faraway-sounding voices.

Beth returned to her studies but with little enthusiasm, and we knew that come fall we would have to get her into a regular school. Stan had stayed in Prince Rupert for the year, building his savings for university. We talked it over with the two of them and decided to rent an apartment near both the university and a high school. We would pay the rent and Stan would buy the food.

Then I went with Beth to register at Victoria High School. The principal was friendly and cordial, but he said Beth could not attend that school because we, her parents, did not reside in the district even though we were paying the rent and she was actually living in an apartment in the district! That boggled my mind. No matter where I turned, I just got the runaround from bureaucrats. Because Race Rocks was in the Sooke district we had to deal with that school board. Finally a meeting was arranged to discuss whether she could attend the school in the Victoria district near the apartment. The minute I walked in and sat down on a wooden chair, alone, facing this long line of faces, I knew they had already made up their minds. They just passed out worthless platitudes until, in desperation, I said, "Will someone tell me what I can do, instead of what I can't do?"

One gentleman who had said little—and I later found out, was a superintendent of the school district—said, "One of the teachers at the Belmont School lives in Victoria. It might not be out of his way to pick her up and bring her back each day." Well, that is what happened. Two teachers took turns and for the two years Beth attended the school, they faithfully took her and brought her back every day. They refused any pay, saying they had to go to the school anyway. We were very grateful.

No sooner had we settled the school problem than Trev noticed the tendons on his hands had tightened so that he could not open them completely. Our doctor sent him to a specialist who recommended operating to remove the sheaths around the tendons. He operated on only one hand at a time. It took a long time for first one hand and then the other to heal and become flexible, but Trev recuperated most of the time at home. He elected to stay on the job as he could handle most duties with one hand (it helps to be ambidextrous), and the junior keeper and I took up the slack.

He could not drive a car, however, and I found out just how good a back-seat driver he could be. I did understand. Once he had nearly lost his life as a passenger in a friend's car during a head-on collision, so that seat was not where he wanted to be. He changed his tune a bit about my driving when his father, who was not given to compliments, told me in Trev's presence what a good driver I was. After a long convalescence—for both of us!—his hands healed. He has had no trouble with them since.

With the station in order, schooling and medical crises over, we had time to appreciate the unique opportunity of living where nature

Scuba divers congregate on the rocks, awaiting proper tidal conditions. Divers came from all over the world to observe undersea life at Race Rocks.

thrived. On this tiny dot of land with a backdrop of the magnificent Olympic Mountains, life teemed below the sea, in the sea, on the land and above the land. Divers from all walks of life and many places in the world came to dive at Race Rocks. The underwater world was opened to us through their eyes. We had explored the shorelines at extreme low tides, but their tales and photographs revealed to us the hidden depths.

Most of the first divers to land on our shores had spears with their equipment, but Trev explained to them that many divers visited, and that if every one of them took just one specimen there would soon be none for anyone to experience. They were wonderful and immediately took to photography instead, or just plain diving. Little did we realize that our concern would be heard a few years later by the diving students from Pearson College. They took up the cause before we left Race Rocks and steered their proposal through all the bureaucratic red tape. The water surrounding Race Rocks was made an ecological reserve in 1980.

From the sea, imposing California and Steller's sea lions gathered together and hauled (pulled themselves awkwardly and slowly) onto the surrounding rocks in the fall. Trev took notes, starting in October 1966 when two California sea lions put in an appearance, followed by eight Steller's in January 1968. He kept a regular count over the years as the numbers increased from a few in the fall, peaked in January and diminished to one or two by May and disappeared during the summer. In November of 1977 he noted 232 Steller's and 126 California sea lions.

We wondered about this increase and speculated that many had been shot by fishermen until a ban on killing all sea mammals went into effect in the late 1960s. We knew there had been a bounty on harbour seals. It had been dramatically illustrated when we looked out our living room window one day to see the barrel of a gun pointing directly at our house—the harbour seals were between us and the hunter. A missed shot would have been a direct hit at us! When we reported it to the RCMP, they told us there was no restriction on shooting firearms in nonresidential areas. I asked them what they thought we were—nonexistent?!

When the army on Bentinck Island practised using underwater explosives, the animals became very agitated and frantically dove into the water, spending most of the time there rather than hauled onto the rocks.

The numbers of sea lions stabilized for a few years, probably because the food in the area would not sustain more of them. When Trev reported and even sent slides of the sea lions to informed sources, showing the Steller's and California sea lions hauling together on the same rocks, he was told that didn't happen. He was not believed until an official scientist paid a visit and confirmed that indeed they did haul together.

One calm day Adrienne and Beth decided to take a closer look at these interesting though loudly bellowing neighbours, and rowed our eight-foot dinghy from downwind toward a group of lions lazily sprawled on a high rock. The girls jumped ashore on the back side of the rock, pulled the dinghy quietly above high water, carefully and silently crept to the top and gingerly poked their heads over the edge to look—straight into the eyes of a two-thousand-pound bull Steller's sea lion just a foot away. They sucked in their breath, stunned. They hadn't realized from a distance that the creatures would be so big, that they would encounter one at such close range. As the girls collected their wits and turned urgently to escape down the high rock to the skiff, the huge mammal, just as startled, also took action and dove straight into the water from his side of the rock.

These noisy winter visitors had to move over a bit for a small stranger who joined the raucous crowd. We peered closely at this new-comer through our binoculars and identified him as a fur seal. He was about a quarter the size of a two-thousand-pound Steller's, yet there he was in the centre of all the hauled sea lions, boldly hissing at anyone who came too near his space. We named him Frosty and watched him doing his thing for eight years until we left Race Rocks. We had hoped he would find a mate and establish a harem in the area. No such luck.

Other mammals vying for space on the surrounding rocks were harbour seals, year-round inhabitants. They sprawled on all the lower adjacent rocks which the sea lions seemed to avoid. The beach visible from our bathroom window was used, as we called it, for a nursery.

Several years in succession we witnessed the birth of a seal. We believe it was the same mother because she delivered her pup near the beginning of July every year. The first time we saw her, she lay on a rock in the bay, acting differently than the other seals, so Trev paused to observe. Before long, the baby popped out and dropped right into the water and surfaced. The mother made soft noises and nosed the infant before she joined it in the water.

Another year she hauled on the rocky beach. We crept down behind a log and waited until finally she gave birth. We kept the

Scientists couldn't believe that Steller's and California sea lions would share the same rocks, so Trev sent out photographs to prove it. For eight years they made room for yet another species, a small fur seal we named Frosty (at centre in this photograph). He was a quarter of the size of the others but hissed threateningly to carve out his territory.

movie camera on her during the pup's birth and also as she slowly and awkwardly inched to the water's edge, urging the young one to come with her, gradually leading it into the water. The sun had gone behind the tower by the time she delivered, so the event was filmed in shadow and it is difficult to distinguish the seals from the rocks. But at least we have a record of the birth.

Many seal mothers and their babies gathered in this area to play in the shallow water, or the babes hauled on low rocks and waited while the mothers went for food.

When killer whales, our frequent visitors, swam into the area the harbour seals became panicky, often diving into the water from the safer rocks. Sometimes a very large group of whales, perhaps eighty, passed on both sides of the island. Other times, small groups of three to eight whales, called transient pods, stayed around the island for a time, hunting seals. We watched one pair of whales split up, surround

145

One of the great privileges of living on the lights was to take in the magic of the natural world, including the always beautiful killer whales. Lightkeepers have been essential to marine biologists and other scientists for their work observing and recording sea mammals and other ocean life.

a hauling rock, frighten the seals into the water and converge on one side to capture their quarry and share the bounty. We had never before seen a killer whale share its prey with another whale.

We were thrilled one week to see a pod of whales with a rare white whale in their midst. At that time, we were reporting any unusual happenings to the provincial museum. After we had seen the whale several times and told anyone interested—we liked to share nature observations—a boat arrived at our wharf with several people aboard. They were interested in whales too, so we gave them as much information as we could. They had just left the wharf when the pod with the white whale appeared. The boat returned and asked to use our radio to call their marina. Before we knew what they were doing, they had a flotilla in the area and herded the pod into Pedder Bay where nets were strung to capture the whales. That white whale was taken into captivity, but did not survive very long.

Some of the whales were penned in Pedder Bay for months. On our way in to pick up mail, go to town or transport family, we stopped at Pedder Bay to visit the whale psychologist who observed and guarded these penned-up whales for eight months. One time I was mystified by a nondirectional airy strange bird song. Finally it dawned on me that what I was hearing was a whale song! These whales in their pen in Pedder Bay allowed us to pat their heads when they came up to us, opened their huge mouths to expose two rows of large pointed teeth and a big red tongue, and waited for a handout of herring. On one visit I bent to pat a whale's head, which felt like a wet rubber boot, then quickly stepped away when the stench of expelled air from the blowhole momentarily repelled me. However, their friendliness drew me back to pat them once again.

At the time we were ambivalent about their captivity, believing that as the general population grew more familiar with whales, they would become more understanding of them. As we saw more and more of the captured whales die in captivity and understood more the distress they must suffer in such confined quarters after having the freedom to range far and wide, it just didn't seem right.

One benefit was the promotion of much more study. Michael Bigg of the Nanaimo Biological Station found a way to recognize individual whales in the wild and began to identify all the killer whales on the coast. He set up a network of whale watchers to alert his research group to any whale sightings so that they could zoom in by boat to photograph dorsal fins, saddle marks and flukes, and identify and catalogue each whale. This research is still continuing. John Ford found he could identify individual pods of whales by their particular pod sounds. He set up a network of hydrophone placements and volunteers for an ongoing research program to track and identify the pods. These men and their assistants and interested observers often visited our place at Race Rocks, and we passed along any info that we could glean. For example, over the years we also saw the occasional minke whale, and once a grey whale. Our awareness of the research sparked our observations. It certainly made our life more interesting as we became aware that lightkeepers are critically important to marine biology studies for on-site data collection and observation.

There were still more kinds of mammals in the sea. Trev rushed into the house one day and told me to grab the binoculars, and we hurried outside to see an elephant seal. I couldn't understand why he wanted me to focus on a huge old "driftroot" that was supposed to be a head, but I dutifully searched for an eye about halfway down the top of the two-foot root floating on the water. Nothing. But when I looked at water level there was an eye looking back at me, and then the animal unfurled its twelve-inch (or longer) proboscis and opened its mouth wide, issuing a guttural rumble. What a sight! We figured for that size of head above water, the body underneath must have been around eighteen feet long.

At other times smaller elephant seals came into the wharf area. One medium-sized fellow heaved himself up the ramp and into the boathouse, lodging himself into a far corner. The surface of his hide was covered with open wounds and we suspected seagulls had pecked away at the open sores. The seal was trying to escape the harassment by seeking some cover.

We let him be, but after a few days the stench from his feces was overpowering. Trev got a stout rope with a loop on one end, lassoed the seal, turned him around and headed him toward the water. Once the seal reached the shore, he gave a huge sigh and laid his head in the water before plunging in and swimming away. We think the poor thing had no reverse gear and did not know how to turn around on land. Trev got out the portable fire pump and hose and liberally gushed sea water into the stinking boathouse.

An occasional Dall's porpoise was sighted at a distance, but when one came into the wharf area we noticed it was badly cut and bleeding profusely, probably slashed by a boat propeller. To save its life, Trev rigged a sling to cradle the porpoise in the water and we tried to contact someone to help it. The animal seemed to know we were trying to help. Eventually a boat came from one of the marinas, but arrived just a few minutes too late. The porpoise died in the sling.

How privileged we were to be enveloped in natural marine life every day—an experience few people have in today's world. Once Trev was accompanied by a group of harbour porpoises on an eight-mile boat trip to Victoria. They flashed back and forth through the bow wave and swam on both sides of the boat, raising their bodies from the water as if to look in on him.

On the land, our dogs got into the act. They would hear the water-animal sounds, rush to the window and stand with front paws on the windowsill to look out. When outside, the dogs raced along the shoreline, barking their greeting to the whales as they circled the island. Similarly, when the sea lions returned in the fall and circled the island close to shore, they snorted a greeting with each rise to breathe, as if looking for the dogs. The dogs barked a return salute.

Other land creatures paid us surprise visits. I was amazed to look out one day and see an otter grab hold of the knotted end of a swing rope the kids had installed, and give himself a few good swings. Not only river otters came ashore at Race Rocks, but also a rare sea otter holed up under the oil shed near the wharf. We found him when the dog began barking frantically at an opening under the shed. When Trev investigated, he was nearly bowled over as the sea otter shouldered his way out past Trev and down to the sea. We wondered if he was one of the transplants to the Washington coast from Kamchatka Island in Alaska, where the United States planned to set off a test nuclear explosion, who had decided to find his way home again!

On another occasion, Les, a friend from air force days, came to visit. He and Trev had become great buddies when fishing the streams in Ontario. Now they were ocean fishing in our boat. Les was very keen to catch a salmon. At the end of a long, unsuccessful day, Trev reeled in his line and Les was casting just a few more times when his line gave a jerk and he yelled, "I've got one, I've got one" and concentrated on reeling in the line without letting it go slack.

Trev was watching the end of Les's line when it suddenly took off, and he said to Les, "It's a duck!" Les turned to Trev uncomprehendingly, still not looking at the end of his line but continuing to reel it in. Trev told him again. By this time Les had nearly all of the line reeled and couldn't believe his eyes. The duck at the end of his fishing line gave a loud QUACK. Actually it was a murre, which deep dives, and thankfully Les's hook had just caught the edge of its wing. They let the frightened duck go, and the bewildered and disappointed Les returned to the island.

We were so spoiled at Race. If ever I wanted a cod, I just asked

Trev to go out and catch one. There is no fish as tasty as one caught from the cold sea and cooked almost immediately.

One day I requested he catch two as I was going to town and wanted to take my mother a treat. He was gone a long, long time. I was reading in the living room, not paying attention to any outside activity, until I caught sight of him in front, but not heading for the wharf as usual. I went to the window to see what was up and as soon as he saw me he waved frantically for me to come. I raced out the door and down to the end of the dock with Trev yelling at me to "Get the pike pole!" As I approached with the pole, he frantically said, "No, no, on the ramp." So I leaped off the wharf to the ramp as he brought the boat in slowly and awkwardly, using only one hand to steer. With the other hand he held the fishing rod and line taut until he could jump out, still pulling the line tight. I knew what he was thinking—she can't use the pike pole for this job and she might let the line go slack. But he finally handed me the rod and said, in a somewhat trembly urgent voice, "Don't let the line slack!" Then he grabbed the pike pole, raced into the water and strenuously hauled a huge halibut onto the ramp.

We had to use the crane with the large hook to lift the halibut, which was the same height and weight as Trev—six feet and 180 pounds—to the loading platform. He had caught it on a thirty-pound test line, one-fifth the usual necessary strength, and had played it for more than two hours before I finally saw him and ran to help him bring it ashore.

We butchered it like a cow and left the skeleton on the side of the wharf for interested visitors to marvel at. The flesh was all perfect, even the underside, and our freezer was full. I slyly reminded Trev that he had not caught two fish.

On land, we continued our close observations of bird life, including a hundred-nest seagull rookery. The nests, washed away every year by winter storms, seemed to be built in the same location year after year so I painted a position mark on the rock for each nest. Sure enough, the next year the nests were right on the same spots. Adrienne still watched over the chicks, three or four to a nest, even though the parents emitted piercing warning squawks at any intrusion.

Trev had quite a time landing this halibut, which was his equal in height and weight. He caught it with a rod (at front) and a thirty-pound-test line.

The gulls warned us of impending storms by spending more time airborne, circling higher and higher overhead and making more than the usual commotion and high-pitched screams.

Guillemots nested in rock crevasses and oystercatchers scratched slight depressions in piles of broken shells to make nests at intervals around the shoreline. We still had the evening circle cackling chants as the oystercatchers flew around and around the island.

Cormorant chicks hatched on east-facing rock where the prevailing wind kept the stench of their droppings away from us. Otherwise, the smell would have been unbearable. Because incubation started immediately as each egg was laid, chicks hatched at different times. One nest could contain nearly full-grown cormorants as well as newborn chicks. Cormorant chicks were certainly not very appealing—no feathers and internal organs visible through translucent skin.

Much more attractive and majestic in appearance were the seven snowy owls perched around our island one year—accidental visitors from the Arctic probably looking for food lacking in their normal territory. Another time a pair of mallard ducks decided Race Rocks was an ideal location to nest. They produced ten little ducklings, but on the first foray into the sea, they all disappeared.

The natural birth-death cycles in the wild applied equally to the domestic animal scene. Adrienne had some goldfish and we built an outside fish pond where they thrived, even producing young, until one day a wounded juvenile seagull discovered the pond and quickly devoured all the fish. He then had the nerve to go around the side of the tower and die! Next trip to town Adrienne spent every penny of her birthday money for twelve new goldfish. Trev put a wire net over the pond and there they lived happily for years, growing larger all the time.

New life came when Adrienne's aunt brought her a kitten. She named him Tulip—the marking on his back resembled a tulip. This fortunate cat ended up with a connoisseur's diet when Adrienne hurried to the wharf, fishing rod in hand, and caught him a fresh bullhead or two.

On the death part of the cycle was Nugget, the dog we had brought with us from Green Island. We had to take him to the vet because he seemed to be in pain. He had an operation for inner ear infection, but it was not successful. He was still in great pain, so we had him put to sleep.

To ease the loss, we found a lively little ball of black fur at the SPCA. At first they wouldn't let us keep her because a vet's examination detected fever, probably indicating distemper. She had really grabbed our hearts, so the SPCA said they would keep her over the weekend and if she improved, we could take her. Again we took her to the vet. He told us that she still was not okay but might respond to careful tender care.

Well, that was right up our girl's alley. The dog was a black spoodle, a cross between a poodle and a spaniel. We named her Crocus, another spring flower. She thrived with hand feeding of raw hamburger and bread crumbs and gradually grew stronger. She developed into a real character. Because she had been lovingly hand fed, she acquired a great fancy for human food, especially if the food was left unattended for a moment. Workmen had to keep their lunches out of her reach or she would sample the contents. She was so gentle, yet showed great spunk for life, maybe because of her faltering beginning.

Later another new resident came to Race Rocks, a tiny bundle of white energy, a miniature poodle puppy. His mother had given birth to six puppies. My cousin, their owner, wanted to find good homes for them and gave us one in exchange for a seascape I painted. This energetic newcomer to Race Rocks, Poseidon Rip Tide (Rip for short), became Trev's shadow.

Changes were happening in the human population as well. The junior keeper was promoted and transferred, and a series of junior keepers was then tried out. The prospects were pleasant people, especially compared to some we had experienced, but mostly they were quite unsuitable. One young man, for instance, was extremely talented in music but could not get the hang of the beacon clocks or take radio messages, even though Trev patiently tried to teach him over and over again. Other prospects came and then, as soon as Trev had them trained, they would be promoted to another station. Others decided it was not the romantic life they had supposed it would be. And so it went...

The old granite dwelling fused to the walls of the tower at Race Rocks is destroyed, 1972. This house had been built in 1860 and was a rare stone building which lightkeepers had occupied until early in 1966. We pleaded with the government to preserve it, but to no avail.

Finally in May 1968, two years after our arrival, Ed and Alice Hay arrived from Ivory Island and stayed with us nine years. Trev and Ed worked well together and we all respected one another's privacy. We exchanged visits by invitation only and then made each visit a special occasion. I remembered how difficult it had been for me years before when I was just starting to teach Adrienne grade one, and the wife of the relief keeper arrived at my door at nine o'clock in the morning and stayed on and on, and I didn't want to be rude and tell her to please leave.

The station was brought up to standard more quickly because of this good working relationship. The old buildings no longer in use were torn down, as instructed by the office staff in town, and debris was cleared away. The large, long, "forge" building presented the biggest problem. It was filled with old paint cans and odds and ends, but finally it too was gone. We did save and store the big old bellows

154

until after a visit from some dignitaries, when we were instructed to send it to Victoria.

The remaining buildings were painted the signature sparkling white with red roofs. One structure that was not razed was the fallout shelter. It had been built of concrete blocks in the 1950s, about eight feet by ten feet and six and a half feet high—a very small room. At ground level one entered a door and rounded a partial wall to find a tiny space with a couple of bunks and shelves. It was supposed to contain supplies and water for two weeks. There were bunks for the two lightkeepers only—I guess the families were supposed to fend for themselves. In any event, it certainly was a conversation piece, especially when we showed visitors around.

The demolition progressed. Trev was asked to tear down the wooden addition (kitchen and bathroom) to the stone dwelling attached to the tower. It dawned on us that the department might be thinking of demolishing the historical stone dwelling also and we talked to them about the historical significance of the structure, more than a hundred years old and one of the oldest granite buildings in the area. We did not know of any historical society. We thought, naively, that once the department was aware of the heritage aspect of the building, they would want to maintain it. Huh! Just recently I learned that since 1982, any building owned by the federal government must be evaluated by the Federal Heritage Review Office before being demolished or altered.

A year later the roof was removed and soon a gang with nothing but a come-a-long arrived to pull the thick stone walls down. No success.

We again pleaded with the office not to tear it down—to repair it and put it to good use as a storage building, radio building or engine house. Our answer was a barge arriving with a bulldozer which ploughed across the newly planted lawns. After many hours' struggle to get a start, they managed to reduce that magnificent building to rubble, gouging part of the tower itself in the process.

A crew then had to be dispatched to remove the jagged bits from the tower with explosives, hire a stone mason to simulate the stonework, and then build ugly metal stairs to the lighthouse tower entrance, now high above ground. It was a very sad day for Race

The Aquarius Diving Club, associated with the Canadian Navy, were frequent visitors to the lightstation. When they emerged from a day beneath the waves, we were always ready to offer hot tea and enjoy their enthusiastic reports from the undersea world.

Rocks. I took movies, but to this day Adrienne has not looked at them. Not only was she old enough to recognize the historical significance of the building, but it had truly been a large part of her life and she was very sad.

The pile of toppled stone and debris was left for Trev and Ed to clear away, and they devised ways to constructively hide the stone by building retaining walls or supports for new concrete walks.

We were surprised at the number of people who came to our shore, but we welcomed them. We always felt that Race Rocks was a rare historic site and as such the property of the people of Canada. We considered ourselves caretakers of history as well as lightkeepers. Any keen person who came ashore was shown around the station and supplied with any history available. These interesting and interested people, from all walks of life, enriched our lives too. They were never the touristy kind, and outside appearances could be very deceiving. One time a couple of kayakers came ashore in very cutoff jeans, long hair and beards—generally very unkempt looking. But their conversation was completely absorbing and we learned they were world-famous mountaineers. They opened the world of mountain climbing to us and they said the visit to Race Rocks had been a rich experience for them.

Now it is interesting for us to look back on the names in our guest book from every province of Canada and fifty-four countries around the world. The number of visitors increased, and soon we were greeting two thousand visitors a year. We made time for them all.

Divers from the University of Victoria, the University of Alberta, the provincial museum, Aquarius Diving Club (associated with the navy), Victoria dive shops, charter boats, friends, relatives, and a *National Geographic* crew came to Race Rocks. Some had their own boats, others Trev brought from Pedder Bay in the station boat. He encouraged the divers to tie up at the wharf to prevent damage to the sea bottom from anchors and to ensure that the divers enjoyed a safer dive. Usually we were ready for a break from our duties when the divers came up, cold and wet, needing a hot cup of tea and a warm place to socialize and exchange information about the undersea wonders they had just experienced.

Occasionally we were lucky enough to experience some things even the divers had not witnessed. I remember the day one of the Albertan divers stood on the wharf and mentioned that he would dearly like to see an octopus. Trev said, "You want to see an octopus? Look behind you!" There was our local nosey specimen slithering up the concrete stairs to have his usual look around.

The *National Geographic* crew came to Race Rocks to film underwater for a day, and they were drawn back many times because they were so impressed with the intensity of life there. One diver with seven cameras on a flexible bar took thousands of underwater photos. The published article was exceptional, and only twenty-odd photos—the pick of thousands—were used.

Cameras also clicked at Race Rocks during the Swiftsure sailing race held on the last weekend of May. The island hummed with activity as we welcomed observers from the Royal Victoria Yacht Club, our friends and relatives, and spectator boaters out to watch the sailboats as they passed the island. It was an ideal viewing location for the original and biggest sailing race on our west coast. The number of race entries increased every year, and in 1982, the year we left Race Rocks, 465 yachts entered the combined Swiftsure and Juan de Fuca races.

What an incredible sight as hundreds of boats set off under sail from Victoria! They rounded the Swiftsure marker at the entrance to Juan de Fuca Strait and returned to cross the finish line the following day, 136.8 nautical miles, testing their skill and knowledge under varying conditions—trying to gain speed in becalmed seas, or reefing sails in extreme wind. When a following wind called for spinnakers, the race start was even more spectacular as each yacht flew its colourful, uniquely designed sail, billowing from its fore.

The make or break of the race was often Race Passage because a yacht under sail could not make headway against the tide at full strength—6 or more knots—even with a favourable strong wind. It was exciting to watch the race from our excellent vantage point, as the boats jockeyed for position in the half-mile narrow passage, often tacking close to our shore.

One year the old faithful Swiftsure entry, HMCS *Oriole*, the 100-foot navy training ketch built in 1921 in Massachusetts, approached Race Rocks. My niece and her husband, who were visiting us from Niagara Falls, had never seen such a ship, so we quickly launched the station boat and raced out to view the magnificent returning veteran. As we waved a welcome greeting, the crew on the *Oriole* released the voluminous spinnaker and the following wind filled it, revealing the colourful giant oriole design representing the yacht's name. Randy and Annie were awestruck, but Randy still had to note about the spray hitting his face, "It's salty!"

Occasionally a boat returning in the dark of night with a weary crew ended up on the surrounding rocks, but the only loss of life occurred in 1976 when *Native Dancer* lost skipper and crew overboard and beached farther up the strait.

Another category of island visitors who came and went were government employees—workmen to do repairs or build new structures, local management to escort visitors or inspect some aspect of the station, radio technicians to install new equipment or maintain the old, the head of the Oceanic Department to give information about taking the daily water temperature and sample.

Political figures from Ottawa even graced our home, especially after a federal election and change of government. I suppose Race Rocks typified what people imagined a lighthouse to look like, and it was close to Victoria by helicopter, so we were on the tour! I remember when Trudeau was first elected and a delegation from Montreal arrived at the station for the tour.

I always maintained a personal policy to treat everyone the same, no matter what station in life, so naturally they all came in for tea. At that time bilingualism was being promoted. Trev helped me clean up after they had gone and showed me an empty package of cigarettes—with no English! Yet all our packaging had to have French and English! This struck us as mighty unfair.

Our superintendent of lights brought an American Coast Guard Commander to visit June 19, 1971, and we listened as this American told our representative how foolish it was to think of automating our lightstations. He went on to outline the problems they had experienced after automation, such as the difficulty of getting technicians to a station if any part of the equipment failed during heavy weather; not having a place or meals available to them if they had to stay on the island; and the challenge of installing new equipment, repairing damage from vandalism, and handling general maintenance—all of which required a crew, which needed food and lodging. All of this made servicing the lightstation much more expensive, and without a lightkeeper to do the regular maintenance, failures happened more frequently.

As well, sight scanning with binoculars to aid search and rescue was not available, which prolonged search and rescue hours. Local weather reports could not be entirely automated. This applied not only to scheduled broadcasts but also to crises. Computers do not make judgement calls. When a lightkeeper was present at all times, most of these problems were eliminated and radio contact for consultation was instant.

We had suspected that automation was in the works for the BC coast, and this visit confirmed our suspicions.

The combination of treacherous waters, low land, surrounding rocks, frequent fog conditions and high winds with blowing spray make Race Rocks a navigational hazards, but also a vital signpost to harbours in Victoria and Vancouver, north through the Strait of Georgia and south into Puget Sound. During our stay at Race Rocks, we welcomed many a party of fogbound boaters.

Our attention was always focused on all aspects of our immediate environment. For example, Trev was very interested in the freighters and tankers plying the Juan de Fuca Strait. A distinctive logo and name were painted on each ship's stack. As the ship passed close to Rosedale Reef, Trev was able to copy (using 20-power binoculars) the design, colours and name of each inbound and outbound vessel. He then organized the information in a loose-leaf binder. Before he knew it, he had three volumes of 609 stacks from freighters, bulk carriers and tankers, with 1,591 names and many ports of registry.

Thirty-three of these ships were tankers and designated as such, but bulk carriers can also be used as tankers from time to time. Some stacks were the same for several names, such as a yellow stack with a broad green band emblazoned with a large yellow O and W. Trev noted seven differently named ships with this stack, most with different ports of registry. He made a notation only the first time he saw a ship so the 1,591 names were not representative of the total amount of traffic that went by.

A few years later traffic separation was instituted for Juan de Fuca Strait. This is a form of "road" using radar to make sure ships entering the strait stayed on one side, and those leaving stayed on the other. Now ships rarely came close enough for Trev to decipher the logos or names, although he still managed to record the odd ship.

Separating ships going in different directions didn't seem to prevent accidents. We began noting these as well. On July 14, 1971 there was a three-ship collision when the *Hoegh Miranda* from Norway, the Danish vessel *Majorgu* and the Yugoslavian *Kosara* crashed into each other in the fog.

In January 1972 the *Doña Anita* sank off Cape Flattery with no survivors. That same month, the *Cap Carmel* lost a deckload of pilings in Juan de Fuca Strait. On February 27, 1972 the *Vall Ocean* grounded off McCauley Point near Esquimalt. The *Van Lene* went aground and was wrecked off Cape Beale March 15, 1972. West of Race Rocks on September 4, 1972, the *Aegean Sea* collided with the *C.E. Dant* and had to be towed by the *Sudbury II*, still locked together, behind William Head where they were cut apart before being towed to a shipyard for repair.

The *Star Olympian* hit a reef at the north end of Vancouver Island January 25, 1973 and much bunker fuel was spilled. The *Vishva Shakti* from India collided with the *Allunga* off Neah Bay May 16, 1973. The *Vishva Shakti*'s bow was heavily damaged, but the *Allunga* had only slight damage.

The British ship *Erawan* collided with the *Sun Diamond* from Japan in Vancouver harbour September 1973, resulting in a heavy oil spill. At 1:00 a.m. December 19, 1973 the *Oriental Monarch* sank five hundred miles northwest of Victoria with a crew of thirty-seven. There were no survivors. On April 4, 1974 we saw the *Pluvius* under tow. At eight in the morning of February 11, 1976 the *Lloyd Santarem* was dead in the water with engine trouble a quarter mile off Race Rocks. It was towed to Victoria.

All these shipping accidents reinforced the importance of safety at sea and our role as lightkeepers. Trev's research indicated ever-increasing traffic, so the problem would only become greater. The big ships represented only a portion of the traffic. Currently there are

161

4,461 licensed commercial fishing vessels in British Columbia, 3,500 registered vessels in the Victoria, Nanaimo and Port Alberni districts alone.

Since we were always present at Race Rocks, boats suddenly lost or disoriented by swift-moving enveloping fog found their way to our shore by following the sound of the foghorn. Many times a group of people arrived at our misty dock through the dense fog curtain, shivering not only from the wet, cold atmosphere, but from fright and apprehension. Often they were wearing only the light summer clothes they had donned for a carefree boat ride from Pedder Bay, sweltering in the heat of a hot sunny day. In summer, while Victoria basks in a heat wave, blanketing wet fog can form in the straits and the unprepared boater venturing out too far without compasses or warm clothing can get caught in dangerous waters.

Just like the Sunday boaters out of Pedder Bay, the crew of other sea-going craft venturing out to the waters around Race Rocks didn't always respect the power and unpredictability of nature, particularly the sea. Fortunately for hundreds of distressed boaters, Trev made himself available to rescue them. Two or three times every week—sometimes even more often—Trev responded speedily to their distress signals at various times of the night or day. They ran out of fuel, were lost, got caught in the tide, were befogged, had mechanical failure, were physically exhausted or inebriated.

Often he received a request from Search and Rescue at CFB Comox to scan the area for a reported distress. With his 20-power binoculars, Trev quickly climbed the ninety-nine steps to the lantern room of the tower, caught his breath and looked toward the reported location of the distressed vessel. From his experience with local conditions and the behaviour of distressed people, he knew the troubled boat was likely not at the indicated position. People in difficulty often saw the lighthouse, then reported that they were near Race Rocks, when they were as far as ten miles away. Others, not familiar with the area, gave wrong compass directions. Even if a crew in trouble gave an accurate position, strong winds and tides could alter their location quickly. To compound the problem, most people did not know how to signal that they were in trouble after sending a radio distress message (like using a hand-held or projectile flare, repeatedly raising and lowering arms outstretched to each side, hoisting an ensign upside down or making it fast high in the rigging, raising an oar tied with rags or clothing, continuously sounding a fog-signalling apparatus, or waving a simple orange-red flag of any size from side to side) so they just waited and hoped help was on the way. Therefore, Trev carefully scanned the sea 360 degrees and applied his sixth sense, after mentally calculating the tide action, wind speed and direction and actions of other boats. Then he hurried to the radio room to send his observations to Search and Rescue.

But most rescues occurred when Trev became aware that someone was in difficulty. When it was safe to launch our station boat, he took appropriate action. On one occasion he was working outside and noticed an inflatable with four divers aboard, preparing to dive from their boat in an area potentially dangerous when the tide changed. So he instinctively kept a sharp lookout, especially since they did not come to the dock. Most divers knew they were welcome to tie up at the wharf and were familiar with the characteristics of these dangerous waters.

It was late afternoon and the sun was beginning to sink when the inflatable started circling Race Rocks, obviously looking for a diver in the water. Trev got his trusty binoculars, hurried to the helicopter pad and searched where the tide was ebbing out Juan de Fuca Strait. Sure enough, about a quarter of a mile toward the setting sun, Trev saw a head and an arm frantically waving as the diver was carried farther out to sea. Trev flagged the circling inflatable, gave the boater the information and told him that he would use arm signals from the vantage spot on the helicopter pad to direct him to the drifting man. The diver was found more than a mile from Race Rocks and pulled aboard the boat just before the sun sank below the horizon. The loaded boat then sped off toward Pedder Bay—without even a wave to say "we're okay!"

Another time when the sea was fairly calm and few boats were around, we noticed a single Pedder Bay Marina boat with a lone male and no visible fishing gear go past Race Rocks at full throttle, in a direct line for Port Angeles across the strait. Trev watched him for a while, but when he reached the middle of the strait without slowing or deviating from his course, Trev reported the incident to Victoria Radio with his suspicion that it could be an escaped inmate from William Head prison at the entrance to Pedder Bay. We heard the operator pass along the information on another frequency, with what sounded like a slight deprecating laugh. The Port Angeles Coast Guard greeted the man as he arrived to dock and held him for the RCMP who, sure enough, returned him to prison. Pedder Bay Marina retrieved their stolen rental boat in Port Angeles and were pleased it had not disappeared forever!

Once when I was "on duty" for the evening shift, alert to weather or unusual happenings, I saw the lights of a boat head in our direction and then home in on our wharf area. Calling to Trev, I raced down to greet this late-night guest. A twenty-five-foot fish boat had already come in on the wrong side of the dock and one of the men, waist deep in water, was desperately trying to get the thrashing boat off the jagged rocks. After much exertion and manoeuvring, Trev and the man guided the vessel to the more sheltered and roomy side of the wharf.

I returned to the house to put the coffee pot on, knowing the hypothermic chill of these waters. When Trev took the men to our basement, I threw down some of his clothes for them to use while their soaked apparel warmed and dried. It was only after I had poured them coffee that I realized we had a couple of drunks on our hands. I made myself scarce, letting Trev continue the shift and deal with the two guests. They begged for liquor, which we did have in the house—but our safety depended on keeping that a secret. Trev had quite a night. Exhausted from physical exertion and lack of sleep, he kindly engaged the men in conversation to keep them occupied until morning.

The next day, Trev checked their boat for any damage, saw that there was adequate fuel and escorted them in our boat to the entrance of Victoria harbour.

A few years later, a group of department workmen came to Race on a job and acted strangely toward us, although we did not know them. Slowly the story came out. One of the workmen had been an expert witness at a Victoria coroner's inquest into a drowning off a boat at Johnson Street bridge. He heard another witness say, "Just ask

Trev at Race Rocks, he is a friend of mine!" It was one of the drunks whom Trev had assisted. I guess the workman wondered just what kind of people we were to have such friends. We told them the story.

Another time we noticed a fish boat wandering in the direction of Victoria, and as it passed North Rock it started going aimlessly in circles. Trev and Adrienne, who happened to be home from school at the time, launched the station boat and headed out to investigate. There was no answer to Trev's calls, so as he came alongside, Trev asked Adrienne to take the wheel of our boat while he boarded the drifting vessel. Inside, a man was slumped over the wheel and incoherent. Trev flung open the cabin door and dragged him outside. Carbon monoxide poisoning seemed to be the problem. The man finally revived and said he was okay, so Trev reluctantly headed him in the direction of Victoria.

On one unusually calm, sunny day we noticed a large cabin cruiser motoring past our island through Race Passage, and stopping suddenly just north of North Rock. Soon Search and Rescue called and asked Trev to take the stationary boat some gas. When Trev arrived with a five-gallon container of gasoline, not one of the six people aboard knew where the fuel filler was located. Trev found it, showed it to them and put in the fuel. He then carefully explained how to get to the nearest marina in Pedder Bay to fill up, because a boat that size would not go far on five gallons of gas. People don't seem to understand that running out of fuel at sea is much more dangerous than on land. These carefree boaters certainly ignored the fact. They continued on to Victoria! Trev patiently notified Search and Rescue that they would soon receive a repeat call from the same boat—again out of fuel—but that he would not make the rescue trip again.

Small craft were particularly vulnerable to sudden weather and sea changes. Two men and a small boy in a ten-foot dinghy with a very small outboard motor ventured near the rocks one afternoon to get a better view of the seals, and got caught in the tide. It swept them toward Rosedale Reef, where there were standing waves (steep and sharp) of about eight feet. They were soon in danger of swamping.

Trev launched our boat and sped out to ease alongside and hand them a line, but instead of wrapping it around something, they hung on by hand. Of course they lost it the minute stress was put on the rope. Trev turned and tried again, but by now both boats were surfing down the front of the wave, barely under control. After nearly capsizing, Trev backed off to less turbulent water as he yelled directions to turn the dinghy at an angle across the face of the waves until they reached our boat in calmer water.

I watched these frightening manoeuvres, my heart in my throat, knowing Trev could lose his life in his attempt to rescue someone else. Finally, with a rope lashed securely to the dinghy, Trev towed them to our wharf and brought them to the house to recuperate. Refreshed and wiser, they returned safely to Pedder Bay.

Another time around Christmas, we looked out to see a two-seater kayak with a lone paddler appear and then disappear in the lumpy seas. The craft seemed to head in our direction, but instead it was carried toward a tidal rip of eight- to fifteen-foot standing waves. The second seat was open to the seas and was filling with water as the waves spilled over the kayak.

Trev and Stan, who was home for the holidays, launched our boat and slapped through waves and spray after the kayak. As they drew near the kayak and cut the motor, one leaned over to grab hold of the low craft while the other helped drag the fellow aboard our boat. Then both Trev and Stan lifted the kayak, turned it over to spill out the water and laid it across the back of the station boat as they splashed through the seas back to our wharf.

The young man in the kayak was the son of our junior keeper, who had taken Hay's place. The kayak incident was truly prophetic and very sad. Years later that same young man lost his life hiking in to see his parents at Chatham Point. The trail to that station was not used in the winter, and it wasn't until spring that his body was found, propped against a tree.

Tragically, not every sea rescue was a success. Out of the mist, early one weekend, a flotilla of boats under full sail surged into the strait from Esquimalt harbour. We were disconcerted to see these twenty-three-foot boats sailing into 40-knot winds and low visibility—mist and blowing spray—that we had been reporting all night. Trev kept the vessels under close surveillance. As they neared Race

Rocks, one after another showed red flares (the distress signal) until thirteen boats frantically waved flares.

Ed came running over to say that from his window he could see the bow of a boat sticking straight out of the water, its full sails spreading helplessly on the surface of the waves. Trev could hardly believe his eyes as he focussed the binoculars on the boat. He ran to the radio room to contact Victoria radio and report the distress signals and sinking boat. Our only means of communication at that time was the AM radio transmitter with just the lighthouse frequency that was used only for sending messages and reporting weather through Victoria radio. We knew the station sometimes turned down the volume on that frequency when they were handling a lot of other traffic and our scheduled broadcast was not due.

Trev tried for twenty minutes to contact someone. The seas were too rough for our sixteen-foot cabin power cruiser. Finally a seiner arrived on the scene. He must have reported the incident on his emergency frequency because soon the Port Angeles Coast Guard helicopter arrived. It hovered just above the waves and let two divers jump into the water near the stricken vessel. When the chopper landed in the trough of the standing waves to pick them up, the waves were so high we could not see the rotor blades.

Four people were drowned, two couples who had young families. The owner, a novice, had only recently purchased the boat and his friends had no sailing experience, but they had entered the cub race from Esquimalt harbour to Port Angeles anyway. Trev was called to give testimony at the inquest and heard how no one had thought to listen for Race Rocks reporting 40 knots all night and morning. Appearances were so deceiving in the harbour, where there was little wind and seas were rippled—it was hard for inexperienced boaters to imagine strong winds awaited them just a few miles away.

After that incident we purchased our own transmitter, licensed to our sailing dinghy. Later, when the system was changed to VHF, we did the same. Then we had receivers and transmitters for any frequency, especially the emergency frequency. We would never again be without direct communication and in such a helpless position.

These few examples of rescues only begin to show the number

and variety of incidents Trev attended routinely, often risking his own life. Without thinking of making a report, he just did it, efficiently and without fanfare. As more and more lightstations are automated, it makes me wonder how many lives will be lost when there are no longer eyes to see and brains to make decisions that are not possible with electronic equipment.

Race Rocks hummed with youthful vitality on the many occasions when Beth and Stan brought friends home for the weekend. The guitars were strummed as singers belted out folk songs, the latest theories on life were tossed back and forth, different courses under study were discussed at length and the Ping-Pong table in the basement was given a good workout. Life for us and Adrienne was quite different when they were away.

Beth was now completing high school, in spite of all the obstacles that had been in the way. We were relieved to know she would have the opportunity to realize her potential. The hassles had been worthwhile! She was encouraged to write scholarship exams, having earned consistent high marks throughout her education. The exams could lead to help with university fees.

At that time young women did not have the same opportunity as today for high-paying jobs that would enable them to support themselves. Beth had already been working part-time through high school as a department store clerk at a minimum wage.

When she was deciding to enter university, she found she had enough course credits that she did not require Math 12, which she wanted to drop. The principal was adamant she continue. He finally agreed to let her drop it after I went again to the university with her to confirm that grade twelve math was not required for the program she would take. But he still insisted she must take a course by correspondence. Oh, for heaven's sake! We advised her to register and work on it if she could, so she took a typing course.

As valedictorian for her graduating class she gave, for that era, an unusual speech. We could hear the breaths being sucked in as she told the assembled crowd that:

We are not leaving a cherished institution to grope our way in the cruel world, as many believe. We are already part of society, deeply entrenched in the happiness and miseries. It is not only the academic learning we obediently regurgitate but it is the experiences which have matured us.

I had made the dress she requested, a white Roman toga with a wide purple band, draped to expose one shoulder. Her long blonde hair was classically styled. She was stunning, but amidst the froth of short puff-sleeved frilly dresses, she did not conform. I could feel the disapproval emanating from the tradition-minded audience.

Beth received the first scholarship awarded in western Canada, let alone a lightstation, in a national competition from the Department of Transport. Because of the level of her marks, she was also eligible for the BC government tuition awards and other smaller bursaries that assured her of being able to continue her education.

Stan had also been busy at university. Busy, that is, except for academics. He applied himself to water polo and the team won the BC finals, which sent them to Montreal for the national finals. He had a large loose-leaf binder full of folk song words and music for the guitar and spent many an hour at sing-a-longs with friends. But after a stint in construction mixing concrete during the winter, he also applied himself most diligently to the academics!

At the end of Beth's first year of university, she found herself a job on a dude ranch in the foothills of Alberta. Trev and I decided to take our holidays at the end of the season and bring her back, also affording Adrienne an experience at a ranch.

Beth was called Lightning. If she completed the cottage work early enough in the morning, she could go with the cowboys on horseback to round up the rest of the horses. With unparalleled efficiency, she did. After her work was finished for the day, she and Adrienne went on trail rides or swam in the pool.

While we were visiting at the dude ranch, some pet gerbils brought by a few little guests produced a litter. Adrienne came to us begging to take a couple back with her. Trev finally said she could take two males. She was overjoyed, and prepared a cage for her babies.

That wasn't the end of the story of the gerbils! Not too many weeks after we returned to the island, we went to town and were away all day. As soon as the boat hit the dock, Adrienne scrambled out and ran to the house. As we came up the walk, the basement door flew open and Adrienne raced out flinging her arms in the air and shouting, "I'm a mother! I'm a mother!" So much for male gerbils!

She asked her father to make another cage so she could separate the pair. He said, "Yes, yes, I'll get to it." One day, not too long after, I went to the basement and a very sombre Adrienne came over to me, holding her hand closed. I asked her what she had there and she looked up at me with such a mournful look. Then she opened her hand, which held some tiny, hairless gerbils. I burst out laughing. Poor Adrienne had expected us to say they would have to go. Instead, Trev quickly built another cage, separated the adults and carefully watched the others, segregating the sexes as soon as identified.

Gerbils are not supposed to live a long life, but those sixteen gerbils liked it at Race Rocks and lived on and on…

That year, 1970, our attention to lighthouse tasks and service was distracted by family events off the island. Stan married and our first grandchild, Jason, was born. He was a tiny premature baby. His mother had had an emergency appendectomy three weeks before he was born, but those three weeks gave him the start he needed. It was tough going for them with Stan still at university and working at one job, sometimes two, to keep the home fires burning.

My father passed away in December of that year and Trev's mother the following spring. We took my father's ashes to Tofino and spread them on his property, and Trev's mother's ashes were scattered in the Beacon Hill rose garden. We still miss them a great deal.

Adrienne was progressing with her studies, but Trev had to take over the math teaching. Although math was my favourite subject, I did not have the talent to get it across to her—she looked at me attentively, but I saw the blinders going down around her brain. It was interesting for Trev—he had to learn "new math" each day before he tried to teach her!

We also realized that soon we would have to get her to a school. She had never been to one, hadn't had siblings at home for some time and had almost never been with any peers. We knew she would have a hard time adjusting to a public school where she would be one of thirty pupils under one teacher, whereas the last eight years she had had two tutors just for herself.

When she was finishing grade eight, I investigated the private schools in the area. We settled on Queen Margaret's in Duncan, where there was more supervision than at other schools. She had led such a sheltered life that we felt this was necessary for her.

September came with Adrienne fourteen years old and about to enter grade nine with classmates for the first time. We set off for Duncan with her uniforms and the very few special things she was allowed to take, like the soft comforter I had made for her from pieces of material used in making her clothes and stuffed animals. Not only would the blanket give her warmth, but each fabric piece had memories to comfort her.

I regretfully drove away from my little daughter, seeming so forlorn and unprotected amongst strangers. Then I cried all the way home, down the mountainous and winding Malahat highway that hugged the shores of Saanich Inlet, to Victoria. I went to visit Adrienne once a week and every time I desperately wanted to bundle her up and take her home again, she looked so sad. I knew she was, but she didn't complain. We felt that if we did take her home she would not adapt easily to the outside world, and her life choices would be limited.

One time Beth came with me to visit Adrienne at school and we both cried all the way home. Finally Beth said, "We've got to do something." On her suggestion and mostly her work, we produced a small booklet with funny faces and funny sayings about crying and such. I knew Adrienne had it beat when she sent in reply a coloured drawing of a blonde-haired pigtailed little girl in school uniform waving goodbye with tears streaming down her face and standing in a pool of tears!

In contrast, Stan was moving forward with his own life and independence. He graduated from university and accepted a position as elementary schoolteacher in Prince Rupert. We were relieved to have him working in a job that maximized his capabilities. We were also sad. Previously he had been available for relief lighthouse work, which meant we got to visit him and his family while he earned money. Add the distance to Prince Rupert and our visits would be limited. So with mixed feelings we celebrated his career start.

Beth came home one weekend with her constant companion and announced they would like to be married in September, at Race Rocks. When she heard of our problem finding a relief now that Stan was not available, she said, "Why can't I do it, Dad?" Women had not been considered as paid reliefs, although keepers' wives were unpaid lightkeepers who filled in many times and ways. Trev thought a bit and said he would present it to the office, which he did. When he was asked if she could do the job, he replied, "Better than most reliefs I have had." So she became, as far as we know, the first present-day paid woman lightkeeper.

With Beth on the island, it was easier to make plans for her wedding. She asked me to crochet her a long peach-coloured dress with knitted panels for the bottom flare. Alice Hay kindly handcrafted the panels. So, with community effort, Beth once again designed and dressed herself unusually and with panache, in a warm pale peach lace gown flowing to the floor, with wisps of sweet pea and baby's breath woven through her long tawny hair.

I filled the freezer with fancy sandwiches and dainties and made the wedding cake. After Beth scouted the shops looking for someone to ice the cake, she said, "I can do better than that." She got books and supplies and produced a professional-looking cake decorated with masses of colourful spring flowers. It was so distinctive and enchanting.

We did have a problem finding someone to perform the ceremony, but finally a naval padre consented to come. Trev with the station boat and Pedder Bay Marina with another boat brought the padre and the immediate families, fourteen people in all, to the island. The sea was a bit bouncy, but there was no fog and the island was bathed in sunshine. It was a unique wedding with the families together and delightedly contributing to the young people's special day.

The next year there was another wedding in the family, this time for Garry. He had gone to Alberta to work and met a young woman to complement his life, and early in the year they sent word that they would be married in February. Good heavens, what a time of year to pick! I guess the weather made no difference to them, and it happened to be her mother's birthday as well as hers. None of the rest of the family could get away, what with exam time and other unbreakable commitments, but Trev and I drove to Medicine Hat although we dislike driving in the winter. We were pleased to be there for Garry and meet his bride and her family.

Having had the experience of four teenagers in a remote place, I strongly recommend more civilization for them at this age. I am grateful we had rich experiences in other venues before our isolated west coast life began. I appreciated that Garry had chosen to live off the lights.

After he left the lightstations, there were long periods when we did not know where he was or what he was doing. He did not write letters and we had no phone. One evening we were listening to the evening news on the radio when the announcer reported a tugboat sinking off Triple Island at the north end of Hecate Strait. The crew had been rescued by another tug, the rescued crew members being so and so, so and so and Garry Anderson. We jerked to attention and looked at each other wondering, could that be our Garry?

Sure enough, he phoned about a month later from Victoria asking us to pick him up at Pedder Bay. It was then we heard how the tug he was on started taking on water and the bilge pumps quit working. The captain sent a Mayday and a larger tug responded. The seas were vicious and the tug could not come alongside the floundering vessel. They wanted the crew to jump in the water and be pulled out from there. Once Garry and the others saw the row of metal teeth on the bow of the rescuing tug, there was no way they wanted to tangle with it while in the water.

As if by magic, the seas calmed for a little while, time enough for the other tug to come alongside the stricken vessel. The crew was told to jump across the space separating them. Garry was the first to go. The adrenalin was pumping. He went to the other side of the deck and took a running leap onto the deck of the other tug, and if a crew member had not caught hold of his pants as he flew by, he would have gone into the water on the other side.

He had been very seasick, cold and miserable, but was taken to the wheelhouse and wrapped in a blanket. As he sat there thanking his lucky stars and getting warm, someone came into the wheelhouse to tell the captain the pumps had quit working. Garry said he put his head in his arms thinking, oh no, not again!

They made it safely back to port and he hasn't taken a job on a boat since.

Garry had always been interested in cars and had put together some very odd contraptions, which were not always passed by testing stations. Once when Trev and I were going to Campbell River on the Island Highway with our camper and truck, Trev turned to me suddenly and said, "Did you see that strange car that just went by with the driver in the back seat?" And then, after a pause, he jokingly said, "I wonder if it could be Garry?"

Soon there was honking behind us. We stopped and sure enough there was Garry. He had a Volkswagen Beetle and had put a V-8 engine in the front. It was so large that it took up the front seats of the Beetle and he drove from the rear seat! Unbelievably, the car operated satisfactorily and even passed the government inspection. (I gather that was a very thorough test by the inspectors. They couldn't believe their eyes either.)

After he was married, Garry was still putting his car ideas to the test. He sent word at the end of July that we had another grandson, named Trevor, and ten days later they drove to the coast in a Model T Ford, painted a brilliant orange, that Garry had resurrected. His mother-in-law accompanied them, thank goodness, because she was there to help with the new baby. She had to scramble over the front seat to the rear seat and sit in the back wedged in with the luggage. Trev helped put a roof rack on the vehicle before their return journey. In spite of it all, the little tow-headed, blue-eyed youngster thrived.

The effect of lighthouse life on the children and our whole family was put into a new perspective when we were approached to appear in our second TV show. I felt protective of our life, as we had had the experience of being misquoted or treated as newsworthy objects, not people. But Don White, who was the whale psychologist observing the captive whales in Pedder Bay, convinced us of his sincerity and sensitivity to our wishes. We trusted him and consented to do a segment for

The lenses that focussed the light beams floated in a massive container of mercury, which sat on a platform rotated by machinery that resembled the inside of a giant grandfather clock. On the wall above the gears are ventilating ports.

"Klahani," a CBC show. It was a fine program and we were glad we had gone ahead with it. He represented us truthfully in our words.

It had been a long time since we had left the lighthouse for a holiday. This year, 1973, seemed the right time. Our experience with the first three children was that after sixteen they would rather be with their peers than family. Also we wanted to take Adrienne across Canada by vehicle, the only way to grasp the diversity and immensity of the country.

Going on holidays meant having someone live in our house and use all our belongings. We felt really fortunate that Beth and her husband were available for this extended period. They were transferring to the University of Alberta and had a couple of months to wait for the transfer. We trusted them to have respect for our household and they knew what was involved with the duties on the lightstation. They were nervous, on the other hand, about my old secondhand wringer washing machine, which leaked water on the basement floor and gave electrical shocks when touched. My priorities had always been for more aesthetic possessions, like an electronic organ. So they came to me and said they had decided that for next year's Mother's Day, Father's Day, birthday, Easter and Christmas they would buy me a new washing machine. Well, that shamed me into buying a new machine. We didn't want them spending their money, meant for university, on our equipment!

I had never had an automatic washing machine, but found one with a suds-saver, important because of our limited water supply. Trev set about installing it. We turned it on and it hopped all over the basement! We tried again—same thing. Frustration. Finally, we had to get the Sears installation expert out. He discovered little plastic feet on the bottom that should have been removed (but there was no mention of them in the instructions). So, after twelve years on the lightstation, I had my automatic washing machine. I could not believe the time saved.

It was our third new appliance. When my sister was building a new home and installing electric heat, she had asked me if I would like their old propane kitchen stove and clothes dryer. We had not considered a dryer because we still had only 5 kilowatts of power between the two houses. When I was a junior keeper's wife I had to be sure I did not use too many appliances and overload the system. Now that I was a senior keeper's wife I was expected to set an example. You just can't win! Anyway, the stove and dryer sounded like heaven.

We asked the department if they would deliver the propane tanks from Victoria, but the answer was no. We went ahead anyway and bought two 100-pound propane tanks. For most of the remaining time we spent at Race Rocks, Trev manhandled the tanks into the boat and rolled them up the hill to our truck and camper, and I drove to the propane place to have them filled. The tanks lasted quite a while, and having the stove and dryer was like heaven, especially when we had to board workmen. And they made life easier for Beth and her husband while we were away.

We set out on our trip across Canada. We visited friends and relatives we had not seen for years and places we had lived while with the air force. I was happy to see Ottawa again in the summer time. Adrienne was more interested in the sights this time than in January 1967. The weather was warmer, and she was now at an age to appreciate the significance of what she was seeing. Of special interest was her first home after she was born, at Foymount, a radar station a hundred miles west of Ottawa. Sixteen years before, on a turbulent, rain-driven night, Trev had driven me to Pembroke, forty miles away, for her birth.

We visited the Gaspé Peninsula, where I discovered three hundred carving establishments and chose a few small treasured carved pieces to take home. We enjoyed a fabulous lobster dinner at a restaurant in Perth-Andover, New Brunswick, which friends had recommended.

Then we headed for Cape Sable in Nova Scotia, where a lightkeeper Trev had met on the beacon course in Ottawa was stationed. We were not sure of the exact location. His mailing address was care of The Hawk, on the southeast tip of Nova Scotia.

We arrived at a tiny village there and tried to get some information, but no one spoke to us. Trev found a phone and our friend said he would be over with a boat in about an hour to pick us up, so we drove to the wharf and sat outside on our folding chairs to wait in the sunshine. Soon strangers sauntered by, nodding or bidding us good day, then stopping to chat. They didn't take to strangers, but once they heard that we were friends of the lightkeeper, they accepted us. Most had never been as far as fifteen miles afield, and they spoke with a very different accent. One of the fellows that stopped told us he wouldn't work for the government any more—why, they took some of his money to pay the Queen and he had never even met her!

Visiting Cape Sable was quite an experience. The job was usually handed down from father to son, and the men tended to marry women from other lightstations. It was a beautiful, fairly large island, and the lightkeeper also farmed. It was one of the few stations in the east that did not freeze over in the winter.

The stations along the St. Lawrence River were now mostly permanently closed as they were manned only in the summer and had not been needed in the winter. Possibly that is why it seems the bureaucrats

177

Stan comforts his four-year-old son Jason, who enjoyed the visit of a grade seven class so much, he wanted to return to Vancouver Island with them.

in Ottawa have so little understanding of the vast open west coast marine environment that is used year round, not just part of the year.

Then we visited Prince Edward Island. Trev couldn't get off it soon enough. He roared around the small island and said "That's it!" He felt trapped, for heaven's sake—after living for years on Green, McInnis and Race Rocks! Maybe the pending ferry strike had a lot to do with his reaction.

That trip, with its many reminders of Canada's vastness and variations, rekindled my enthusiasm for and curiosity about the larger world—and my zeal for visitors, with their hidden wisdom, experience and special character.

In June of 1974 Stan began the tradition of bringing students to visit Race Rocks. His grade seven students had seen little outside Prince Rupert, and he wanted to expose them to different lifestyles and a larger perspective, in the hopes of inspiring the thirst for more knowledge. The students did not value their education and saw no point staying in school. At that time a young person could get a job without an education and earn as much money during a summer as Stan earned for the whole year teaching—after spending all those years and dollars getting his education.

The school board did not help financially with the field trip, so Stan suggested the students raise their own funds, collecting bottles, having a fair or raffle, or whatever. He acquired his licence to drive a bus and rented one to drive them to Victoria. The children raised some of the expenses and prepared a budget. To cover the rest, they organized work parties for cooking meals, doing dishes, cleanup and other jobs. Stan arranged for rental boats from Pedder Bay Marina and put a capable student in charge of each boat. Trev went to Pedder Bay with our station boat and escorted them to Race Rocks.

Thirty-one students with their gear and supplies were quite a houseful. They slept spread out on every floor and we stepped lightly between the bodies for necessary trips between rooms. A long lineup for the one bathroom slowed the preparations for breakfast, but they were an enthusiastic and well-mannered bunch.

Trev had brought Jason, Stan's son, and his mother to the island earlier and the little four-year-old was asleep when the first group of young people came ashore. When Jason had first begun to visit the island, I started a tradition of keeping a supply of large cookies in the freezer, iced with his name. When he woke from a deep sleep and saw his "dad's kids," as he called them, already ashore, he went without a word to the basement, got one of his special cookies and stood on the porch with it, taking small bites, as if to say: You may visit here but this is my territory!

The first evening the students sat on the floor in the living room, singing the songs that they had composed in poetry class and Stan had put to music. There was silence soon after they settled for the night— with no horsing around or late-night gab fests. All the girls adored Stan and all the boys tried to emulate him—he had it made and didn't have to enforce strict discipline!

The students certainly were exposed to a different lifestyle: no car at this home, no corner store, no community centre or movie theatre, but lots of wildlife, fresh air and freedom to run outside and improvise games not impeded by traffic.

We then had the opportunity to broaden our own horizons by spending five days cruising on a beautiful ketch built by Trev's brother Jerry. We had been aboard many times but never away from the dock. The sails stayed furled. Not even a puny breeze ruffled the tranquil sea as we putt-putted peacefully along. On our return cruise there was no wind, until—eureka—some puffs ruffled the water. Jerry and Trev whipped the genoa sail from its bag and yanked it aloft to slowly fill, billow out and push us across the rippled sea gently and silently when the motor was shut off. New feelings were awakened in us as we glided along under an azure sky with wisps of summer clouds, and the reflected sun sparkling like diamonds off the sea.

After our sailing adventure, we drove to Tofino and indulged in a delightful, spontaneous side trip to Lennard Island that reminded us of the inauguration of our atypical lifestyle. The day was idyllic at Chesterman's beach near Tofino, and Lennard Island was only a half mile away. We launched our trusty Peterborough canoe (we always carried it with us on top of the camper) through the now gentle beach surf and waded out to climb aboard. Adrienne sat in the more stable bottom centre, I settled at the bow, paddle in hand, and Trev pushed off and climbed in the stern to steer and power-paddle swiftly to the island.

The old house was gone. In its place was a brand new house similar to the one at Race Rocks. The island had more landscaping near the houses with pockets of flowers protected from the wind on the inside faces of the hills around the houses. We did not have time to explore our named trails—the wind was rising—so we quickly boarded the canoe and returned to Tofino, digging the paddles rhythmically and energetically, tucking away a satisfying memory of our quick visit to Lennard Island, our first lighthouse station.

Our main purpose in visiting Tofino this trip was to look at our property, a share of which had been left to us by my dad. We wanted to see if it was feasible to work on it now in preparation for the day that we would retire there. Seeing the rugged west coast land made us realize we could not do much in a week, or even a month or a year.

At the time we didn't connect these two significant events, sailing and rethinking our Tofino property, but the seed that was planted grew slowly, and took over our lives for the next twenty years.

That fall, as Trev and I were having a cup of tea in the living room at Race Rocks, he said, "What would you think about building a boat rather than a house?"

"I don't know," I replied hesitantly. "Let's talk about it."

We talked about the property in Tofino and acknowledged that building on it was out of the question as long as we were on the lights. We remembered our days aboard the sailboat with Trev's brother and the feeling that a boat could be a real home, as well as a way to travel. All of our children would soon be moving away. The more we talked, the more it seemed a good idea.

We decided to proceed with more plans. I told Trev that the boat would have to be a real home—I did not want to camp the rest of my life. And it had to be seaworthy in case we wanted to go far afield. Finally, it had to be beautiful—that was important to me.

Taking the first step, getting the plans, started us on two decades of commitment to a project that absorbed most of our free time and energy. Trev's brother Jerry took us to visit a marine architect on an island off Canoe Cove near Sidney. The architect kept us talking for a long time. I guess he was trying to figure out whether we knew what we were getting into. (We didn't.)

Trev had not done any boatbuilding, but he was skilled in many types of construction and could read plans and books. The architect asked me about my approach. I told him how I, an untrained person, had confronted the intimidating task of teaching a six-year-old to read and write. I had tackled only the work for one day and didn't look any farther ahead until that part was complete, and I felt the same method could work for the boat project. Eventually he sold us the plans.

Jerry told us a long time later that the architect was prone to give different sets of plans to different types of people—some for the dreamers, some for the starters but not finishers, and some for the doers. I still don't know just what type he figured we were!

We sold the property in Tofino, and this allowed us to accelerate purchases for the completion of the boat. Before, we had bought only as we could afford, never going into debt, except at the very beginning, when my mother lent us $2,500 and we had repaid it right away.

181

From then on, everything (except the money for Adrienne's schooling) went toward the boat—even holiday money. We took no time off for seven years, choosing to put those resources in our project.

But at the beginning—oh boy! Where to start? We were told to get the boatbuilder's bible, *Chapelle's Boatbuilding*. But we couldn't understand a thing, we had to learn the vocabulary first. Somehow Trev studied and thought and used his ingenuity and lofted the plans (drew enlarged plans onto quarter-inch plywood).

The logistics of figuring what materials would be needed for each step, locating a source, and getting them to Race Rocks seemed insurmountable at times. The Department of Transport put up more hurdles. They had issued occasional memos suggesting ways for lightkeepers to develop hobbies and use their free time to keep up morale, but when our project became known, they immediately notified us that we had to have written permission and that we must guarantee removal at our own expense if necessary. Trev wrote the required letters and received permission.

Fortunately we had a full basement in our house, so Trev had a good-sized area for winter work. He finally found a local mill where he could get special fir lumber for the keel, and dead wood (large chunks of wood shaped to form the boat forward and aft). He had to laminate the wooden part of the keel, as he could not fit large slabs of heavy lumber in our sixteen-foot boat. As it was, he had to transport the thirty-three-foot 2x10s lashed to the sides of the station boat cabin to balance the boat, carrying only two or four at a time. And so it went for the whole project.

We decided that we would work on the boat every day to keep the momentum going, even if it was only for twenty minutes. We did not look ahead to the finished product, but concentrated on the immediate work. I was able to take over much of the lighthouse work and enjoyed mowing the lawns and doing other physical exercise.

Meanwhile, we had more visitors to Race Rocks every year. We always managed to fit them into breaks, and to take anyone interested on a tour of the island and into the house for a cup of tea and visit.

Most of the visitors from Ottawa were federal government men, but one time a man's wife came along. She was very interested in lighthouse life from a woman's point of view and kept asking all sorts of questions. I tried to fill her in on what it was like to raise children in this situation. Not long after they had gone, we got a message from the office. What had we told these people? We couldn't understand what the flap was about. Then it came out that the wife had been astounded at how little help we had had educating the children. I was asked to write a letter explaining the difficulties we had encountered. I did just that. In spades.

Not too much later, policy was changed and we received some financial help. Not retroactive, but a little for the last few months of Adrienne's education. We were glad to know that other parents could select the most appropriate education for their children, and get assistance for it.

That school year, 1974-75, we had our first visitors from the new school in Pedder Bay—Pearson College, a United World College, officially opened April 19, 1975. The purpose of the college was to bring together students from all parts of the world, on scholarships, so that the young people could learn to understand one another and thus promote peace.

In February 1975, three students stayed with us for their project week, and different ones came every year until we left in 1982. We enjoyed the sparkle of these bright, idealistic young people from different countries of the world and from Canada.

At other times, the diving classes from Pearson College did their sea dives around the Race Rocks. Ongoing studies such as logging underwater life in grids and creating a database took place there. The students also installed and monitored a current gauge in Race Passage that eventually was used to establish a new category, Race Passage, in the tide tables for southern BC.

The project most meaningful to us was the designation of the Race Rocks area as an ecological reserve. We had wondered what would happen after we left. The new keepers might not be as aware, interested or protective of the natural life surrounding Race Rocks. The young people heard this concern, probably supported some by the biology teacher. Without our knowledge, they did the research and took it through all the phases of government procedure, and Race

One of the best things that happened during our tenure at Race Rocks was that the island was designated an ecological reserve in March 1980. Garry Fletcher, a biology professor, is at front with a bottle of champagne. Standing, left to right: Trev, me, and two students from Pearson College in Pedder Bay, Johan from Sweden and Jens from Denmark.

Rocks was declared an ecological reserve on March 28, 1980. Pearson College became its warden on our departure in 1982.

Our contact with these young people and the teachers at Pearson College was very rewarding and we hope they gained another perspective by working with us.

For all the years that we had struggled to give our children the best opportunities for education, we were rewarded that year by Beth and Adrienne. In the spring, in Alberta, Beth earned her bachelor's degree with distinction, having been on the Dean's List for two years, and was granted a graduate scholarship. Adrienne's graduation in June was also special. She was a lovely young woman who had overcome many obstacles to reach this point of taking control of her own life. When she had started school we knew her academic standing was fine, but socially the school environment was more of a challenge. Adrienne was never picked to join a sports team because she lacked experience. But by graduation, she was recognized for her participation in all teams—field hockey, badminton and volleyball. She had learned stable management and horseback riding, she excelled at swimming, and she joined the choir and drama group. She revelled in all of these activities and was presented with the school pin for "most improved." Most people take education opportunities for granted, but after our experience on the lights, we viewed public schooling with a new sense of appreciation.

Back home again, Trev continued to find an hour here and there free from lighthouse duties to work on the boat. A name for the vessel was evolving. Trev wanted a name that he did not have to spend twenty minutes spelling if we were ever in trouble. Jason, our grandson, called us WaWa and BaBa—water and boat. Occasional songs had grabbed me, such as Frankie Laine singing "I will go where the wild goose goes." (I could just imagine myself winging along with the wild geese.) WaWa meant Canada goose in Ojibway, so we agreed on WaWa. However, I did not think it was a very beautiful name for such a beautiful design, so we compromised on WaWa the Wayward Goose.

When we went to reserve the name, the very nice and polite registrar told us that he could find no one to challenge the name, but we would have to wait to see if any had come in since the last list had been published. I said, "Who would want WaWa!" He could hardly keep from bursting out laughing. Later the name was confirmed and then it felt more real.

I asked Jerry where I might take sailing lessons. He said, "Flo, the best way to learn is in a dinghy." We had a sabot—a small eight-foot sailing dinghy—and I bargained with Trev that if I got the plans and he made the mast, boom, rudder, tiller and centre board, I would make

When Trev and I decided to build a fifty-seven-foot boat instead of a house, Trev's brother told me the best way to learn to sail was to study the basics and go out in our eight-foot dinghy and try it. And that's just what I did.

the sail. He made them all, but I couldn't find sail material to fulfill my part of the bargain. We ended up buying a sail.

The dinghy was ready, but was I ready for that cold, cold water? We took the water temperature every day and I knew it did not vary more than ten degrees, winter to summer. It stayed near 45 degrees Fahrenheit and if I capsized the dinghy, it would be hypothermically icy. Trev had a wet suit, so one fine day as the tide went to slack and a very light breeze wafted, I struggled into his wet suit. (It took longer than planned as my lumps were not in the same places as Trev's.) I then got in the dinghy and learned that the sheet controlled the sail and the tiller would steer the boat if handled properly. I was on my own as the line was released from the wharf. Trev had put the station boat in the water as a precaution. Away I went with the wind, concentrating on the sheet to control the sail and trying to co-ordinate the tiller. Whoops. The tide had turned to ebb and I was carried out to sea with not enough wind to tack against the tide. Trev came alongside with the power boat and handed me a line. What to do? I only had two hands. I put the sheet between my teeth and with one hand steering the tiller and the other hand holding the line from the station boat, I was towed ignominiously back to the wharf. Eventually I learned to sail the sabot, and I can say I am the only woman to have singlehandedly circumnavigated Race Rocks in an eight-foot dinghy!

This newfound independence of mine became crucially important some months later. Trev was launching the boat to return a visitor to Pedder Bay, and he saw the tender leaving Victoria with supplies for Race Rocks. Trev rushed Sylvia and me to Pedder Bay and returned alone and in a hurry to start the winch motor in preparation for offloading the supplies.

I finished my business in town and called on Stan and his family before heading back to Pedder Bay. As I came in, he told me to sit down—Trev was injured and in the hospital. We drove straight there and found him in the emergency ward with blood pressure readings scribbled all over his pillow—readings that looked really low to me. Trev later wrote a letter to friends describing what had happened:

February 26th. A grey and miserable day. The tender was due to unload some gravel sacks sometime in the forenoon. I took Flo and Sylvia quickly across to Pedder Bay and returned immediately as I saw the tender leaving Victoria.

The winch and winch motor had just been replaced with new equipment. I was not completely familiar with the new installation and it did not properly fit in the winch house. It was too large for the small house and left no room to get to the other side of the engine without stepping across the chain drive gear between engine and winch. By noon we had only offloaded one load due to a combination of problems. While the workboat was taking a lunch break, or so I thought, I went to the house to put on more warm clothing, including wet weather pants over gumboots with extra socks, and grab a sandwich. Just as I started my sandwich, I saw the workboat returning so headed back to the winch house to start up the motor again. When the crew had left, someone had thrown a rope snotter into the winch house and after starting the engine I noticed it was resting on the exhaust system which had not been insulated, and posed a threat of fire. I stepped over the winch gear to retrieve it. Unbeknownst to me, the motor clutch did not disengage when in the

187

disengaged position. I realized this when the cuff of my wet weather gear was slowly pulled into the winch gears. The throttle and shut-off button were on the opposite side of the motor, out of my reach, but I managed to reach and slam the two decompression levers. The motor slowly ground to a halt but not before my foot was in the gears.

The workboat was on its way to the wharf and through the open window I frantically waved and yelled. They genially returned the wave, but could not hear above the noise of the workboat. When finally docked, they realized something was the matter and came to the winch house, but no one knew what to do.

Trev told me later that the pain of his foot in the gears was excruciating, but he willed himself to stay conscious. He was afraid that if he was found unconscious, the boat crew would try to start the engine to release his foot, not knowing the clutch was malfunctioning, and that his whole leg would be pulled through the gears.

By this time the junior keeper arrived. He and I discussed the situation. There was no reverse on the winch so if the motor was started it would just take my foot in further. Another solution was to take the winch apart, which would take considerable time. We decided that, if at all possible, the drive chain should be pulled backwards with some sort of lever. When Ed, a smallish man, knew what needed to be done, he took hold of the chain and with a mighty jerk, back it came far enough to get my foot out. At a later date both Ed and I tried pulling together on the chain drive and could not budge it.

After my foot was released, I asked if anyone had first aid. The answer was negative. I did a quick check myself. The bleeding seemed to be minimal so I felt I was not bleeding to death. Ed got extra coats and made me as comfortable as possible on the floor of the winch house. It was now snowing outside. The mate was in radio contact with the *Camsell*, which had a helicopter on board, and I felt confident that I would be taken off immediately and flown the few minutes to Victoria and a hospital. What do you know, someone decided I should wait the two hours for the Search and Rescue helicopter from Comox. Not only that, but they wanted to take me to the helicopter pad to wait OUTSIDE

This photograph of Race Rocks, taken in 1970, shows how compact our "neighbourhood" really was. The wharf is at lower right, and just left of that is where we built our boat, the WaWa.

IN THE SNOW so that they could continue offloading the gravel! I said "NO," I was staying put until my injuries could be attended or taken to medical care. Not one of the crew had any first aid. My shadow, Rip Tide, did not leave my side.

The Workmen's Compensation Board later condemned the whole winch setup. Some of it was rectified. At least guard shields were put on all the gears and working parts.

Trev's heel bone was crushed, but the Achilles tendon was intact. His whole foot was lacerated and looked like an argyle sock of stitches when put back together. It was bandaged heavily and after a few days he was sent home until the bandages could be changed. During that time we put our house in order for a relief keeper. We knew it was going to be a long haul, and the prognosis doubtful.

Over the months that followed, gangrene set in in some places and there were many weeks in hospital of debriding with bleach and eventually skin grafts—some took, some did not. Trev progressed from a wheelchair to crutches. When he could get around on crutches we went home. The department had changed their policy and I was now allowed to take on the job of relief lightkeeper—with pay, no less—enabling us to stay in our own home. There Trev's recovery accelerated, but he could not get back to the boatbuilding. He would putter around in the basement, aimlessly going from one thing to another. I didn't know how to help. Months later the day came when he could walk again. He had not lost his foot, but the scars are there still and he must wear special shoes.

Trev's brother Jerry was a shipwright. Whenever he and his wife came for a weekend visit, Trev was able to get expert advice on building the boat. On one beautiful fall day I talked to Jerry about Trev's lack of direction since his accident, and Jerry suggested to Trev that they lay the lofted plans on the concrete top of the water cistern, and cut the harpons (shaped 2x10 planks that locked the top of the ribs to the deck perimeter). They completed the cutting that day and from then on Trev was again focussed on the slow, methodical work of building our boat.

Some time after Trev's accident, a memo was issued to all lightkeepers, ordering that "Lightkeepers will not stick their feet in winch gears."

After Trev's accident I had to become more self-sufficient. I had never taken the station boat to Pedder Bay on my own, although I was familiar with its operation, and I did not have the strength to raise the motor should it malfunction. We had a rule at Race Rocks that the boat was watched as it left the station until it disappeared into Pedder Bay, so that help could be called if necessary, but I did not want to be the cause of such a call.

One day a few months later, Trev became ill enough to go to bed on his shift—something he just never did, even though he knew I could hold down the fort. I had not had a chance to read a new book, *First Aid Afloat*, that Stan had given us for Christmas 1978, but when Trev went to bed, I read the book through. All except the chapter on "amputation at sea"—which, I thought, I'll only read if I ever have to deal with it! I took Trev a cup of tea and asked him a series of questions about his condition. As he answered, bells started ringing for me, fresh from my medical reading. I said, "You know, listen to Dr. Anderson, I think you have appendicitis."

We could do nothing at night, but with the first streaks of dawn, Trev, bent over with pain and struggling to stay on his feet, slowly walked with me to the boathouse where I released the cable on the drum so that the boat carriage slid on the tracks to the water as I raced to the wharf, catching the lines when the boat floated free. Painfully, Trev inched himself aboard as I heaved to release the motor and lowered it into the water. Then, with a press of the starter button, it roared into life the very first try and we sped off to Pedder Bay on an unusually calm January sea. The hill from the wharf in Pedder Bay seemed like a mountain as I helped Trev to the truck. Urgently I drove the twenty-five miles right to the doctor's office.

The doctor told Trev he usually didn't make a diagnosis without a blood test, but he was quite sure he had appendicitis and it would be faster for me to drive him to the hospital than to wait for an ambulance. He would phone ahead for blood tests and a surgeon. At the hospital, Trev was whisked to an operating room. Eventually the surgeon informed me the appendix had come out before it burst, but only just. By March Trev was mobile again and fit enough to resume his duties and his work on the boat.

As always, change was on the horizon. Ed Hay, our junior keeper, wanted to retire a bit early and set the date for August. For weeks he joked that for his retirement dinner, the department was taking him to...the Golden Arches!

Trev and I decided to have a Race Rocks fun party for the Hays. For days I prepared fancy tea sandwiches, decorated dainty cakes and tarts and froze them, ready for the big do. For this gala event, I went to McDonald's and acquired a bunch of their coffee spoons—the plastic ones with the tiny spoon on the end. We stocked up on pink champagne, cleaned the silver and laid out the crystal and china.

We made a gold watch for Ed from the ends of bleach bottles glued together and painted gold, with a plastic screw on top, numbers out of order with crooked hands on the front and a flowery inscription on the back. We elaborately gift-wrapped the "watch" for presentation on the big day. To show our real appreciation of our years together at Race Rocks, we also bought silver goblets inscribed with his lighthouse service record—for a later presentation after the spoofing.

On that special day, with the help of the pink champagne, we all became quite mellow reminiscing. Trev slipped into the bedroom to don his straw boater hat and hang a sign around his neck reading LOVEABLE LARRY in large letters. He was poking fun at the District Manager, who had trouble remembering names. I don't think there was one time during the nine years Ed was at Race Rocks that Trev was not asked, "What was his name again?" So Trev came into the living room and made a speech, standing first on one foot and then the other and mentioning the fine work of John, Jack, er—Joe, George—er—Dave.

Just as the fun was escalating, a helicopter landed on our helicopter pad and out stepped the District Manager, the Deputy Minister from Ottawa and his executive secretary. Trev whipped off his sign and hat, hurried to greet the party and took them on the usual tour of the station while I prepared another pot of tea. As they came in the house, one remarked that it appeared we were having a party. I said, "Oh yes, we're celebrating Ed's retirement and all the local residents are attending." Only the executive secretary twigged! After they had gone, Trev reminded Ed that he was the only lightkeeper to have a deputy minister and district manager attend his retirement party!

After the excitement of the retirement party, I needed a new challenge. I had always had an itch to do things right from scratch, and now I got a bee in my bonnet that I would like to gather wool sheared right from the sheep, wash and card it, and then spin and knit the wool into garments. First I needed a spinning wheel. With a photograph to guide him, Trev creatively built a stylish working duplicate from pieces of driftwood. (Later I found out that wheel was designed for spinning flax rather than wool.)

Next I needed raw wool. My sister-in-law knew someone on Salt Spring Island with sheep and I got my sack full of wool. It needed to be washed, and when we dumped it out, we realized just how badly it needed washing—it was all the clippings from around the posterior! Undaunted, we spread the wool on the sunken garden lawn. Trev donned wet weather gear and, hose in hand, proceeded to fertilize the lawn. God, what a job!

With determination, I tried the time-consuming job of hand

carding the matted wool, but finally, reluctantly, sent it to Vancouver to a professional carding establishment. The wool came back soft and ready for spinning. Then I knitted it into toques with individual names as Christmas gifts for the family.

Trev's work on the boat continued, and I decided to enroll in a celestial navigation course at Camosun College in Victoria. It was tough just getting to the classes. As usual, I had to leave Race Rocks the day before and return the day after the class, making it a three-day-a-week course. But I thoroughly enjoyed getting my teeth into something so mentally stimulating, and the knowledge proved valuable in the years to come.

Near the end of the eight-month course, the instructor told us to bring our sextants and he would talk about them. I had bought a cheap plastic one which I used to take sights from Race Rocks. I usually came within .8 mile of the exact location at Race. Of course there was no heaving sea, but the horizon was not always the best. It was often hard to distinguish from the mist against the land.

The day came for the talk about sextants and I trundled off to class with the precious plastic sextant in my briefcase. I was about to take it out when the instructor brought forth his treasured antique sextant and lovingly caressed it as he told us how useless was a plastic one! I did get up courage to ask what he considered a good sight. He said anything up to three miles was considered accurate. Well, I thinks to myself, the plastic sextant hidden from sight was not so bad after all.

With the course finished and a new year started, I was ready for the beginning of a steady flow of visitors. In February two students from Pearson College came for their project week—occasionally finishing essays, sometimes practising sailing in our little dinghy, but most often learning about lighthouse life and observing the natural environment at Race Rocks. Scuba divers from the college revelled in lengthy underwater adventures. During this time the more proficient of the sailors often fulfilled their goal of sailing against tide and wind to Race Rocks and then returning to the college in Pedder Bay.

Stan had decided to give up teaching elementary school in Prince Rupert and take a position at Camosun College. He taught there for six years, continuing his practice of bringing his students to Race Rocks for a weekend, especially to dive and experience the abundant underwater life, to learn how to deal with tricky tides, and to see the big mammals hauled on the surrounding rocks. Frequently the sea lions dove in the water to swim with the divers and look at them curiously underwater, blowing bubbles near their face masks.

At another time, Stan and a friend, who was also an experienced diver, decided they wanted to test the tidal stream at full strength underwater. While the tidal river yanked at their fingers when they grasped a rock, the force of the rushing tide vigorously pulled their masks off their faces if they tried to stay in one place, making it impossible to hang on.

In February 1973, another teacher from a local school, Fritz Karger, rented boats from the marina to bring his students to the island on the first of several yearly trips. Children always were intrigued with their visit and gave us new insight, especially when they sent thank-you drawings of the life at Race Rocks. One of them showed our house with one window coloured red. We finally figured that one out. The red shade on the hanging lamp over the dining room table glowed red through the window. These students were very curious about the inside of our home.

Work on the boat progressed methodically. With a cumbersome and dangerous band saw, Trev cut eighty (plus a few spare) ribs from the bending oak planks we had packed in rock salt to prevent drying. An acquaintance had asked us to keep the home-built 24-inch band saw with wicked blades that needed frequent sharpening—or expensive replacement if bought individually. Trev bought rolls of bandsaw blades, cut them to size and welded them to fit. One time a blade broke as it was slicing through a plank, sending parts of the blade in all directions. He found pieces on the other side of the oil shed that had flown right over the building. Luckily no one was around that side of the building at the time and the blade had not flown at Trev. After bravely persevering to cut the solid two-by-two-inch ribs from oak planks, he then hand-planed them smooth on all four sides. The laborious and time-consuming effort of creating and using temperamental saw blades, slicing eighty ribs and hand-planing

every surface gave us a glimpse of the monumental task we had chosen to undertake.

In the spring, Jerry visited again. Trev and he wheeled from the
basement the ungainly completed dead wood bolted to the laminated
keel. Balancing this massive weight at one point on one dolly meant
that two men could move the unwieldy forty-foot chunk by themselves, although it had to be coaxed around corners and over rocks and
took many hours to move. Then they set it up on the concrete pads
Trev had previously dug into the lawn below our bedroom window.
Jerry stayed long enough to help Trev set up the molds, wooden forms
placed upright on the keel at four-foot intervals that determine the
shape of the hull.

Trev scarfed (cut on a slant and fitted together to form a better
join) two-by-three-inch twenty-foot pieces of fir to make some forty-
foot lengths called ribbands that reached from bow to stern longitudi-
nally. Then he bolted them to the molds over which the ribs were bent
vertically so that they had the correct shape to form the hull of the boat.

Then it was time to think about bending on the vertical ribs
(much like the shape of human ribs). To accomplish this, we used a
special fifteen-gallon steel tank with a pipe attachment to a steam box.
The tank, full of salt water, rested on steel bars raised off the ground
with huge rocks. Underneath we lit a fire and then stuffed the ribs in
the steam box to heat. Trev had previously cut notches in the keel and
we had clamps hanging on the ribbands ready to clamp on the ribs to
the ribbands. A come-a-long (a mechanical device used for cinching)
was ready on the top of the boat to bend the ribs over the ribbands.

When each rib was hot, Trev smothered one end in tar, ran with
it to the boat, stuffed the end in the prepared notch and spiked it in
place. Then he climbed to the come-a-long and gradually pulled in
the rib as I clamped it to the ribbands.

We could do about four in a day, and all went well until we started on the stern, which had a much sharper bend. One day we broke
four in a row and gave up. Trev thought he would have to laminate the
ribs from thinner slices rather than use the two-inch-square ribs, but
he decided to give it one more try on another day. We couldn't believe
it. Four went on almost like spaghetti.

That evening when we tried to figure out what was different, the light suddenly went on. There had been no wind. That constant wind was cool enough to chill the ribs between steam box and keel, so that they broke rather than bending. From then on, we only did ribs for the stern on calm days, which wasn't often.

It was refreshing to take short breaks away from boatbuilding to talk with an ever-increasing number of student visitors arriving in their lasers or dive boats. One day, as we walked some students down to the wharf and their boats, we saw an entire group of killer whales, about eighty, surging and porpoising rapidly toward us in the strait. A few stopped to perform leaps and to slap their tail flukes on the surface as they dove out of sight and rolled a few times, passing on all sides of Race Rocks. What a magnificent sight!

These students had come in lasers—craft that are close to the water with little freeboard—and one of the lads said he didn't like the idea of sailing through the whales into Pedder Bay. He was genuinely afraid. We told him there was nothing to fear, that we had been through them time and time again without mishap. He was still apprehensive, so Trev put the station boat in the water and the nervous lad in our boat, and towed the boats to safety in the bay.

In 1975, the loyal pen pals in Australia that I had started writing to twelve years earlier, finally traversed the globe to visit us at Race Rocks. First was Jeannette, from Tasmania. On her second visit in 1978, she stayed with us in windy weather, which normally meant no unexpected visitors. We could relax, visiting while peeling pears garnered from Mom's tree in Victoria. Trev was resting in the bedroom, and I automatically scanned the waters regularly for anything unusual.

Once when I glanced out, I saw a sixteen-foot cabin cruiser slapping through the moderate sea and spray toward our wharf. Yelling for Trev, I rushed to the dock to take the lines from Jack, my cousin's husband, who had three poodles in the boat: Rip Tide's mother Baby, and siblings Shy Guy and Bulldozer (both aptly named). Earlier we had volunteered to keep the dogs at Race Rocks while Lil and Jack attended an important function. The wind was rapidly rising so Trev told Jack to put the dogs ashore and scoot back to the bay before the seas became too dangerous. Mission accomplished, Jack turned to speed away and I scooped up one dog I thought was Shy Guy, but—oh no, Shy Guy had jumped in the water and was swimming after the boat. I captured the other dog on the wharf and ran to shut him in the basement as Trev grabbed the pike pole and managed to manoeuvre the errant dog gingerly ashore. By this time I was back on the dock, and as the terrified wet and slippery poodle landed on shore, I tried to grab him, but he eluded me and sped away. The chase was on. Like a comic strip, Shy Guy dodged one way around a building to evade us. Just as we thought we had him cornered, he slipped out the other side to race to another place, performing the same "catch me if you can." Finally Trev, after many unsuccessful tries and armed with his big salmon net, caught him. Through the net we saw the poor pooch lying utterly terrorized, showing only the whites of his eyes as Trev reached to grasp him firmly and hurry to the basement.

We got our exercise that day, for sure. Fortunately, Shy Guy didn't get pneumonia and he eventually warmed up to Trev, just a little. When Trev came into the house from giving the weather or some other duty, the five dogs, our two and the three visitors, ran to greet and clamber all over him. Years later, Jeannette still chuckles as she reminds us of the "dog show."

My two other pen pals and their husbands—Gwen and Ron from Melbourne and Joy and Keith from outside Melbourne—also came to visit. It added another dimension to our friendship to have face and voice in the picture and they, in turn, could experience firsthand the special conditions of life on the lights.

Joy and Keith understood particularly well. I went to Vancouver to pick them up, and on the journey back they realized we were not only on a tiny island, but we had to get there via another larger one, Vancouver Island. This highlighted for them the isolation of our life.

In between visitors and dramas, the boatbuilding went on. We were now ready to plank the hull of the boat. Fortunately a friend, Blaney Scott, told Trev of a new product on the market called cold cure epoxy glue. This glue could be used in temperatures as low as 4 degrees and was not affected by dampness. These were the two worst problems we had at Race Rocks.

We had 10,000 linear feet of red cedar specially milled, stacked

197

and tied in bundles making a pile about four by five feet of varying lengths. The strips were one inch by one and one-half inches, convex on top and concave on the bottom so they could fit together snugly like spoons. These planks had to be scarfed and glued for a stronger join, as none was forty feet long. Glue was brushed on the plank ready to be installed and also on the plank already in place.

We worked together, me smarming on the glue and then holding the plank horizontal while Trev used his trusty hammer to drive two-and-one-half-inch spikes through two planks and into the third. Previously I had chalked all the nail placements so that he would miss the nails already in. Being the careful crafter that he is, Trev had only two nails in the entire hull go off line.

As I worked, I had plenty of time to think. First I calculated how long it took us to do one plank the entire length of the boat: one hour. That meant we expanded the finished hull one inch in one hour. Then I wondered how many inches we needed to apply to each side: one hundred and twenty inches each, or two hundred and forty for both sides. Two hundred and forty hours to plank the hull! As I watched Trev hammer the spikes and I gently bent the plank, I thought: how many nails per plank? How much did they weigh? How many bangs with the hammer would Trev make before the hull was finished? At least a hundred and fifty thousand, allowing only two swipes per nail and one to set!

Winter was around the corner, so Trev drilled holes in the rocks and installed steel cables forward and aft of the skeleton of our boat. Then we covered the top with plastic and nailed sixteen sheets of quarter-inch plywood over that. During the first storm I heard rip, crunch, rattle—it sounded as if the whole boat was being torn asunder. In the morning we collected only a few pieces of the plywood strewn about the island—the others are likely still in orbit—but the boat itself was intact. When the wind abated, we got some three-quarter-inch plywood (three times as thick as before) and Trev spiked the sheets securely to the top molds! No more trouble.

The new year—1977—began with an unusual greeting. Trev found a bottle on the shore with a note inside—what a twist finding a bottle while *on* a deserted island! We tried reading it, but it was in a language we could not even identify. Trev spread the note on the dining room table to dry. When the helicopter arrived with a work crew and pilots, we asked if anyone could decipher the note. None could, but they said to wait for Coke, the flight engineer, because he could figure it out if anybody could. When Coke took a look at the message he exclaimed, "Can you believe this, it is written in my native tongue, Yugoslavian!" He translated the note from a lonely sailor on one of the freighters heading out to sea on Christmas Day. He missed his family, but wished anyone finding the note greetings for the coming year.

That year there was more construction and destruction going on on the island—we were building and the Ministry (formerly Department) of Transport was destroying. The big old engine house with the tall fog tower was torn down and replaced with a small flat-roofed concrete structure. That distinctive tower had rectified the "silent" foghorn problem back in 1920s. The story goes that after a number of shipwrecks and near misses in the fog, angry mariners blamed the lightkeepers for shirking their duties. But soon it was discovered that the lighthouse tower and surrounding rocks deflected the warning blast to a whisper. The solution was to put the horn high in the air so it could be heard at great distances. Now it was gone and the new horns, installed at ground level, once again could not be heard at sea. I suppose someone assumed the electronic age, with all the new instruments for navigation, was all that was necessary—horns were obsolete. Or maybe it was short-sightedness on the part of government.

Careful examination and planning should have been applied when the engine house was torn down. Most of our usable water had run off that roof to collect in the cistern. Now we had a small, flat-roofed area that the seagulls used as neutral territory—a place for all to gather and visit—and they completely fouled the top of it. Some time later the health inspector took samples from our cistern and said it was the most contaminated water he had tested. Luckily, we never drank water straight from the tap. The incredible chemical strength of seagull excrement became clear to us when gulls began using our boat deck as neutral territory. The droppings even took the cuprinol (a green wood preservative) from the plywood.

After years on the lights I could have given government planners a few other tips as well. For one thing, our house was designed for city living, not lighthouse living. The bedroom windows were at chest height, and as we were forever on the alert for unusual noises, we ended up climbing in and out of bed numerous times at night to check the view.

On one of the rare days Trev went to town, I was rattling around the house when the light went on for me. If I can't move the windows down, I thought, why not move the bed—up!

No dillydallying around for me. I whipped down to a pile of left-over concrete blocks, loaded a bunch into a wheel barrow, carried them to the bedroom and put my idea in force. It worked like a charm. I made it just high enough that it was still easy enough to climb into bed, but from a resting position I had a panoramic view. Great! Then I made a long, long bed skirt and I was in business. Jason, our grandson, loved the new arrangement. He used the space under the elevated bed for a cozy playroom!

As for the power system, there was always a problem regulating the output, so there was usually inadequate power for the houses. At one time the ministry decided to split the power for domestic use and the power for the station, which required different sources of power and the installation of six diesel engines, two for domestic, two for station and two for the foghorn.

First, the station had only the main light, a few other light bulbs, radio beacons and radio transmitter, so it needed minimal power and there was little or no load on the engine. To rectify this problem the powers-that-be installed a large resistor to burn off power—a huge waste of energy, as it had to be outside to dissipate all the heat it produced. And, if two irons were used at the same time in different houses, the engine would shut down.

When the domestic power finally was increased substantially, we were not supplied with the electrical appliances that it could now handle. During a visit from the District Engineer, when I served my usual hot, fresh-from-the-oven coffee bread, he noticed the sad state of my old decrepit propane stove and asked me if I would like an electric stove! I was amazed as I said yes. We were nearing the end of our tenure on the lights, but I thoroughly enjoyed what time I had with that stove—baking bread was now a joy in a cool summer kitchen, and preparing meals was less time-consuming.

The efficient quick cooking method also gave me more free time to work on the boat with Trev. It was really taking shape now as we finished planking the hull and started the decking with two layers of plywood.

We wanted to build our own masts, but found we could not buy any of our own Sitka spruce grown on the Queen Charlotte Islands— we would have to import it from either the United States or Japan! We finally located a wonderful spar maker in Vancouver and contracted him to make the two masts for our ketch.

Maybe life was getting too easy, with all the modern conveniences and our flourishing progression on the boat, so I had to produce my share of excitement.

One day we had a crowd ashore and were showing them the boat. Earlier I had scrubbed the deck of seagull leavings and had put a sheet of plastic over the unfinished cockpit hole. Jason, our grandson, came with me as we clambered up the ladder to the deck.

Trev had been positioning the molds for the cabin and had not secured the aft mold, but I didn't know this. I grabbed the loose mold with one hand and it gave way. I plunged inside to the bottom of the boat in what seemed like slow motion. It could have been worse—my head and neck narrowly missed the engine bed—but I broke both my arms. That put me out of commission for a few months, although I could still do most of the household tasks with plastic bags over the casts. I couldn't help with the boatbuilding so I spent a lot of time taking movies of the life cycle of the gulls.

The delivery of the new Perkins diesel engine for the boat was the next big shipwright challenge. It just was not possible to get it to the wharf in Pedder Bay, nor to bring it across in the station boat. It was the only time we asked the department for help in bringing supplies for our project, and they agreed. After the engine arrived on the sea truck, Trev rigged up an A-frame with a cable dangling from the deck of the boat to lift the massive engine upwards with a come-a-long, and slowly inched it to the aft part of the boat. He pulled the

A-frame away so that the engine cleared the hull, then gently eased the A-frame forward and lowered the motor into the boat onto a piece of plywood. He then shoved, pulled and wiggled the engine and plywood forward gradually onto the engine beds.

Construction moved ahead methodically, slow but steady. Trev hand-planed the hull, first at a 45-degree angle one way and then the other way. I then sanded and sanded and sanded, starting with coarse 40-grit through to successively finer grits to 120. It was the same for painting. We applied several undercoats, sanded between each coat and eventually applied enamel. The boat was taking on a fine look, sleek and finished.

There were advantages to being novices and unconventional nautical people. Rather than take the prescribed direction, we could find our own solutions to problems as we faced them. For example, my accident made us even more conscious of possible accidents at sea. Trev had extended the cabin and offset the companionway entrance, leaving little foot room on the deck between the companionway entrance and the cockpit. We thought this might be dangerous in a rough sea, so Trev rounded off one corner of the cockpit to give a much more secure footing on the deck at the entryway to the cabin. He also offset the steering column so that the helmsman would not be directly behind the mizzenmast. These untraditional solutions worked very well.

The next stage in construction was building the keel. We could not bring a lead keel ashore on the island so the architect designed a concrete keel that we could construct. One day our good friend from air force days arrived from Sooke with two tons of iron balls from a crushing mill, in steel barrels lashed inside his boat. He had been a pilot in the days when he and Trev flew in the Arctic dropping supplies, so he knew all about lashing down goods in a moving transport. The iron balls would be ideal for the concrete keel.

Trev made a form, lashed rebar to the keel bolts for a cage to contain the balls and old window-sash weights, iron rods and a steel shaft that we had collected—9,000 pounds in all. He completed the plywood form surrounding the lot, cut holes to pour in the concrete and filled the form with concrete using a pencil vibrator to eliminate any

Trev and I take a break with our dogs Rip and Crocus, 1980. Construction of the WaWa (in background) was proceeding slowly but surely. (Jim Ryan photo)

air spaces. Stan organized a work party for that job, bringing the cement mixer, concrete and volunteers all in the Pearson College dive boat. A splendid effort!

One of the perks of working high up on the deck of the boat was the good view all around. Trev had not had time for any fishing for a long time. One day while on deck, he saw a big Steller's sea lion catch a large salmon, tossing it about and losing sight of it as it lay on some kelp. In a flash, Trev was on the wharf with the pike pole and had the eight-pound salmon ashore. The sea lion looked frantically for his salmon for some time! We had that salmon in the freezer when a long-time friend contacted us and came for a visit. I don't know which he enjoyed more, the salmon or the story.

In September 1980, we took a breather from the boat project to prepare for our youngest child's wedding. Once again the special community effort of family and friends made Adrienne and Jeff's wedding meaningful and unusual.

Adrienne wanted to be married in the little log church at Queen Margaret's where she had sung in the choir. Jeff had a friend who drove a double decker bus and as a wedding present, he volunteered his services and his bus to take the guests from Victoria to Duncan.

I made the cake and Beth did a unique job of decorating it. I did not have the time to prepare a reception, but we had a wonderful windfall—a share of my benevolent Uncle Cecil's estate.

We chose the Empress Hotel for the reception. The wedding guests had a fun time getting acquainted on the bus ride over the Malahat summit to Duncan and back. The reception at the Empress was really classy, with elegantly served gourmet meals on finely set tables.

Winter was again with us and we tackled the teak decking for the boat. We purchased the wood raw and in large quantity by combining our order with two other buyers. It all had to be cut and trimmed, so Trev rigged up our bandsaw, as its thin blade would produce more planks rather than more teak sawdust. Each plank had to go through the saw four times: once to cut a half-inch board from a twelve-inch plank; then to trim each side; and lastly, to cut one edge a saw-kerf narrower so that when the boards were butted together on deck a pronounced seam was left to be caulked with paraseal. I helped by holding one end of the ten- or twelve-foot plank steady. The perimeter boards for the deck had to be hand-shaped to fit the contour and vertical slope of the rails.

Working so hard on the details of the boat, we lost track of our overall progress in construction. Then Beth came to Race on one of her infrequent visits, bringing the stained glass doors she had designed for the cabinet in the dining area. They were beautiful. One had a Canada goose flying over a backdrop of Olympic mountains, and the other showed Race Rocks. Beth came out to the boat, sat on the companionway stairs looking around, and then said, "Gosh, I think you are going to finish it." I was stunned. I couldn't believe one of ours would doubt it. I knew others would and did, but one of ours? Never! Well, at least these two points—the glass doors and her comment—made us realize we were getting there!

After Beth departed, a group of diver friends from the provincial museum finished their dive and came up for a cup of tea. I was carping to them about that daughter of ours even thinking such a thought, and one of them spoke up and said, "Now Flo, don't be too hard on her. I once worked in the sale-of-plans department for Sampson Company, designer of cement boats. For every thousand inquiries we received for plans, a hundred bought, ten started and one finished." It's a very good thing I didn't know that when we started. I might have had doubts myself. As it was, once we started, neither Trev nor I ever doubted we would finish.

1981 was a hectic year—so much to do in so little suitable weather. We decided to hire help to lay the teak deck, and we engaged a splendid craftsman and experienced sailor, Pete Watson. He anchored his boat in Pedder Bay and came every morning to Race Rocks in his Zodiac to help lay the teak decks. What a job! Trev said they just looked at the paraseal (a synthetic black rubber in which the teak planks were laid) and it stuck to their eyeballs. It was a tedious job, smarming paraseal on the deck plywood and one side of a plank, fitting the plank snugly in place and then countersinking and screwing in the stainless steel screws. The eighth-inch-wide seams, half a plank deep, were then filled, using a putty knife to force the paraseal firmly in the seam.

Once the paraseal had dried, the whole deck was sanded level. My job was to glue and hammer teak plugs in all the screw holes—thousands of them. Trev and Pete finished the deck and Pete fitted trim for the transom and installed the finished stanchions and taffrail. With two men working well together the job was finished in two weeks—record time.

Just as in our experience with the teak decking, we were able to find a trustworthy person to do the wiring. Dave Calland, a Ministry of Transport workman and navy friend of my cousin, volunteered to do this important job for us. We enjoyed his company and we appreciated his generosity.

Sometimes lighthouse life outside the regular duties intruded on our concentration on the boat. For one thing, the Superintendent of Lights decided to give us a hard time about the boat, saying that we didn't have permission, etc. He had given written permission nearly seven years before, and fortunately we had filed the letter and could produce it.

Then our junior keeper was promoted to a better location and a new one arrived. This fellow, a big bruising sort of guy, stepped out of the helicopter and as he started down the ramp, without a how-de-do, asked Trev when he was going to change the shift! In inclement weather he took the station boat to the mainland—on his shift and without notice—and stayed away for the day. Generally we found him arrogant and belligerent. Eventually he resigned, and we were relieved.

Nothing could stop us now. We were more impatient than ever to be away from all hassles. By now it was time to think concretely about launching the boat. Trev asked the owners of a barge sporting a long crane at the navy dock in Pedder Bay about the possibility of lifting our boat off Race Rocks. One of the engineers looked at our situation and said it could be done, but the job would be easier if the boat was moved twenty feet closer to the water. We brought a boat mover to Race Rocks and he moved the boat with rollers and come-a-longs. Then we strategically wrapped boat straps around the hull—ready for the crane to grasp for lifting—and put extra water pumps aboard in case the hull leaked.

Everything was ready. As soon as the job in Pedder Bay was finished, the barge with its crane was supposed to detour to our island to lift *WaWa* into the water. One day we saw it heading out, towed by a tug. However, it didn't turn toward our island but kept right on moving toward Victoria.

Trev finally went ashore and phoned management in Vancouver, who told him they were willing to send the crane barge to our island, but Seaspan tug would not take them anywhere near Race Rocks—it was too dangerous. We complained to the Seaspan office in Victoria, because their tugs had removed boats from rocks around our island and had even came ashore at Race to borrow Trev's tools, and to get supplies and help. But the visit did us no good. Next Trev inquired about a helicopter, but the only one that could lift that much weight would have to be brought from California, at a cost of ten thousand dollars.

Early in 1982, when we were ready to launch the WaWa, Trev and I towed a set of fifty-one-foot rails from Pedder Bay to Race Rocks, with empty gas drums as floaters (above). When everything was ready for the launch, John, the man in charge of the move, reminded me that something could still go wrong. Oh, no! Seven years for naught? Beth chose that moment to take my picture (below).

So it was back to our original plan—from seven years before. Trev had chosen this flat piece of lawn adjacent to a beach that, with modification, could be used to launch a boat. In the soft soil he had laid concrete pads that kept the boat level and correctly positioned while we built it. Over the years, he had built fires on the rocks leading down to the water. They cracked when the cold tide water covered them, and at the next low tide Trev smashed and moved them. Now the beach was fairly clear of large rocks except for some unmoveable bedrock.

One of the chaps from the yard, a demolition expert, offered to set some charges and blast the rock that had to be removed. Low tides occurred at midnight, so in the black of night the blasting expert and a friend arrived and set the charges, and I bet I'm the only one to have such a big blast for my birthday, December 30. It did the trick. After the smoke cleared and the broken rock was removed, we had a clear launching ramp area.

Then we contacted the moving company that had moved the boat the twenty feet. They were interested in such a great challenge, but concerned that the workmen would be stranded if the weather fouled. Not to worry, we had room for them to stay with us until the boat was launched. It was old hat to me.

The men spent four days making a set of rails to slide the boat on its cradle across the beach to the water. Trev and I, one in the station boat and the other in the Zodiac in tandem, towed the rails to Race Rocks at slack high tide and jockeyed them generally into place. On the morning of February 7, 1982, *WaWa* was ready to go down the greased rails. As the day dawned, tranquil and glistening, family members arrived. Stan manned the Zodiac (to fend *WaWa* off the end of the wharf and assist with tow if necessary) and Janet arrived with Jason, now aged eleven, wide-eyed with excitement. Beth had her camera at the ready and Adrienne and Jeff had more cameras. Four boat movers stood by, one with a cutting torch in hand to sever the last remaining cable and allowing *WaWa* to plunge into the water, her natural element. Waiting in the water was Rob Waters from the marina, with his powerboat ready to tow us to Pearson College because our insurance did not cover starting the engine on land and we could not

February 7, 1982: the launch was successful. We were floating!

risk trying to start the engine in water for the first time in this unpre-
dictable area.

I was donning my fluorescent orange cruiser suit in the house
when John, the head mover, found me and said, "Flo, I've got to tell
you something. We have done all we possibly can but you must understand that something could go wrong." I stood there thinking, Oh,
God—and my mind flashed back over the seven years of hard work
that could be for naught! Beth snapped a very telling photo.

All was ready. I smashed the champagne across the bow, wishing
WaWa fair winds and a following sea, then climbed up the ladder with
Trev to sit in the bottom of the cockpit with my legs braced against
the back because John said there might be a jolt when the boat hit the
water. I was ready! The red ensign we had taken down from the flagpole at Green Island wafted from the bow and the cameras clicked as
the mover with the cutting torch sizzled the cable holding us to the
land. I waited for the jolt. None came. Then I felt a rocking motion
and leaped to my feet crying, "We're floating!"

We were on cloud nine. What a mixture of emotions—joy, relief,
excitement and some sobering thoughts that the job was not finished.

After it was launched successfully, the WaWa was towed to Pedder Bay by the marina boat (above), with Rob Waters at the helm. (B. Cruise photo) At the Pearson College dock, we were welcomed by many hands to our home port.

But as *WaWa* actually glided on the unnaturally still water, all that seemed unimportant and we savoured the moment.

Stan accompanied us in the Zodiac and Jason was lifted aboard *WaWa* to share the joyous experience. Many glad hands ran onto the Pearson College wharf to herald our arrival and grab the lines we threw toward the wharf. Champagne flowed on board, while at Race Rocks the gang celebrated with more champagne and a big pot of spaghetti. It seemed anticlimactic returning to Race Rocks, leaving *WaWa* at the Pearson College dock—our home port—as inscribed in a book given to us by the director of the college.

We had one last big task, to return the launching rails to Pedder Bay. That was some trip. I was elected to tow the rails, afloat with empty gas drums, in the station boat. Trev, in the Zodiac, would tow the cradle. I started out all right, but was soon caught in the tidal stream. There was no way I could control the rails trailing behind as the tide swept me toward Victoria, not Pedder Bay. Frustrated, I had just about decided that, okay, I would go with the tide to Victoria, when Trev finally saw my dilemma and tied the cradle he was towing to some kelp. Now, with the two boats in tandem, we successfully pulled the unwieldy launch tracks to the marina in Pedder Bay. I felt better when I was told that no one boat could have steered against the tide, but two boats could control the tow.

We had not taken holidays for a long time and Trev had a lot of accumulated leave. We decided to take a hundred days' leave to see if we liked life aboard our new movable home before taking early retirement. So the packing and crating began again as we stored our trunks, boxes and crates in the basement. Trev had more than forty years of government service with the combined air force time and twenty and a half years on the lightstations—sixteen years at Race Rocks.

On March 2, 1982 we left Race Rocks to begin our new life. There was no time to reminisce about the two decades we had spent on the lightstations. We immediately revelled in the freedom of living aboard the boat and soon decided that this was the life we now wanted to embrace. Trev's retirement did not take effect until late September, but we did not return to Race Rocks except to arrange for our belongings to be removed from the island.

The WaWa, ready for action.

Over the next thirteen years we explored almost every island, cove and inlet on the BC coast, and Puget Sound, the South Seas and New Zealand. Sailing a fifty-seven-foot boat across the ocean and maintaining our vessel and ourselves was a full-time occupation, but Trev and I did eventually take time to reflect on our two decades as lightkeepers.

We certainly learned a lot about the daily work of maintaining lightstations, and about the profoundly important responsibilities of lightkeepers—official and otherwise. We find it distressing to say the least that the Canadian government has decided to automate the west coast lights, and that our rugged, convoluted, 16,900-mile coastline—2,000 miles of it on Vancouver Island alone—is gradually becoming bereft of manned stations. After 137 years, our coast may be left without protection—except for machines.

Our twenty years "keeping the light" taught us that staffed lightstations are important to all kinds of vessels plying BC waters; thirteen years living aboard the *WaWa*, navigating the inlets, bays and islands from the southern tip of Vancouver Island to Prince Rupert and the Queen Charlotte Islands, have convinced us that staffed lights are absolutely essential.

We depended on the lightstations particularly for local weather—much more accurate for particular areas than general forecasts—in order to plan the next leg of a voyage, to wait in or to seek out a safe anchorage if the forecast or present weather was unsafe, or to pick the optimum window of favourable weather for a safe journey. We depended on the stations' foghorns because electronic equipment could and did fail. Once our depth sounder quit as we hugged the shore near Sooke, trying to follow a safe fathom line in the fog. I stood on the bowsprit listening for the sound of old faithful Race Rocks' horn to guide us through these treacherous waters. Our radar gave out between Hawaii and the entrance to Juan de Fuca Strait, and on the same voyage, when we ran into difficulty off the Oregon coast, a tiny cockroach moved into our ham radio and lodged itself in front of the sensor for changing channels.

Any of the 3,500 Victoria, Nanaimo and Port Alberni registered vessels and thousands of licensed small and large pleasure boats could experience these relatively minor problems or many worse ones—to say nothing of what could befall the large commercial tankers, freighters, cargo and cruise ships, or the 4,461 licensed commercial fishing vessels. Automated equipment can and does fail on the lightstations, and without lightkeepers to monitor and replace or improvise or report quickly, marine traffic of all types and sizes is endangered unnecessarily. Computers and machines simply cannot produce local weather reports the way a skilled human being can. And without lightkeepers, Search and Rescue lose an adjunct for surveillance and quick action rescues—instant radio communication to scan for a reported incident, immediate response with a station boat to nearby disabled craft (hypothermia can occur in less than twenty minutes), or quick reporting to Search and Rescue of likely craft in trouble.

A Canadian pilot told us that for the same reason—that electronic equipment aboard ship can and does fail—they must be able to handle the ship in any event and thus have always relied heavily on foghorns, beacons and local weathers from the lightstations. These pilots guide 4,800 foreign vessels to and from Vancouver through Haro Strait every year, 300 northbound and 275 southbound cruise ships through the inside passage, 40 to 50 ships both ways using Cape Beale, and 40 to 50 using Triple Island. Within the compulsory pilotage area, that amounts to 13,000 trips a year.

Lightkeepers also provided an important link for scientific data collection—sampling water, observing tidal changes and wildlife patterns, recording any unusual natural occurrence—on a long-term, all-weather, year-round basis. This ongoing information gathering is now also lost. Scientists, students and interested citizens are not likely to be on site when something unusual happens.

Besides giving us a much deeper understanding of the vital role lightkeepers have played on the west coast, lighthouse life has had many influences on all our lives—influences that are still revealing themselves to us.

After teaching elementary school and college students, Stan started his own business, still teaching but now on anything to do with water safety. Diving was a special avocation, and he taught scuba diving for several years. In May 1985, he married Janet, who became an

The WaWa *sails from Suva to Latoka, Fiji, 1986. We enjoyed thirteen years exploring every nook and cranny of the BC coast and Puget Sound, and we went on to sail the South Seas to New Zealand.*

integral and active part of the business. Jason, Stan's son, is married and works as a computer programmer with his own business in Vancouver. Janet and Stan attended Jason's wedding with their new daughter, Mikayla, six weeks old. Having spent two consecutive teen years in an unusual environment, Stan believes his entrepreneurship, and his relationship with his wife as marriage and business partner, were shaped partly by the independent and co-operative lifestyle Trev and I shared. Both he and Beth took on great responsibility at a young age—living away from home in high school and later working to put themselves through university.

Beth, with five years' isolated west coast adolescence, is still our free spirit determined to taste all aspects of life that she can reach. She sees her strong self-motivation and independence, especially in developing her own unique business and artistic expression, as a result of her early self-educating and self-entertaining environment. She attended university for eight years, then went to technical college for carpentry, graduated with honours and opened her own carpentry business. She played soccer for ten years with vim and vigour, taught windsurfing courses in the summers, joined Toastmasters for a few years, honing her skill as a public speaker, and used her skill as freelance photographer for weddings and graduation groups. Her New Age thinking and alternative lifestyle (country living by herself, with no TV or newspapers and a short work week) seem to have their roots in her unusual teen years. Adapting to a materialistic society after growing up without stores, advertisement or peer pressure has been a struggle at times. Ironically, Beth chose display—visual merchandising or retail advertisement—as a way of tackling the issue head-on. Her business specializes in designing and decorating store windows, and lately she is developing her artistic side with her usual zeal and dedication.

Adrienne, who spent ten childhood years insulated on islands, is sensitive, insightful and open-minded. As a mother, she intuitively guides and supports her little boy, Ethan, with gentle wisdom. Growing up with two parents who lived and worked side by side, at home, may have influenced her choice of mate—a partner who shares equal responsibility for parenting, earning income and doing household chores. Adrienne and her husband Jeff have both worked at Butchart Gardens since their marriage, occupying one of the Garden's houses during the last few years. They combined their passions for diving and horse riding by making a bargain that if Adrienne became a diver, Jeff would take riding lessons. That pact has enriched both their lives.

Garry lives in Alberta with his wife and three boys, who are now treating him to the teenage years. With his wife's support, Garry has been able to build and race stock cars and has won some races. He was put out of commission for a while when he fractured his back in a race accident, but he recovered to race again. Personally I am glad I do not live near enough to watch the races. It would be too scary for me!

For me, the first stage of transition to lighthouse life was dramatic. There was an immediate plunge into reality and maturity, perhaps similar to the experience of young men who went off to war and came back mature men, telescoping years of development into a short time. My extreme idealism and naivete were slapped down hard, especially when I met our first neighbours. My goodness, I thought, those fictional characters in books actually exist! But as Trev and I and our

Trev and I celebrate our fiftieth wedding anniversary, 1994.

youngsters immersed ourselves in the adventures of our unusual life, I found strengths I had not thought I possessed. We tackled each new problem together, gaining confidence as we found successful solutions.

The life suited Trev very well, although he too had expected less harsh conditions—both mental and physical. It was better for him than city life, with its streams of confusing traffic and masses of people. He could live the "outdoors life" and fling himself into physical projects that gave much satisfaction, bringing order out of chaos.

Both Trev and I appreciated the unique and, for us, unprecedented opportunity to observe and study our natural environment. We could watch nature at work with almost no influence from "civilization," playing out the timeless cycles and rich patterns of life. We were always there when any unusual bird or mammal appeared, and we experienced weather in all its different phases, including the legendary west coast storms, which few people can observe in safety.

Trev and I believe that if it had not been for the twenty years we spent in this unique lifestyle, we may never have thought of building the *WaWa* or sailing off in it to see the world. We learned so much during its construction, and it gave us so much freedom, challenge and pleasure after we left the lightstation. All the hardships we had endured on the lights had developed the strength, knowledge and confidence we needed to begin this even more daring, nomadic, sea-going life.

Most of all, the lighthouse life knit our family together, and we are grateful for the close ties that continue today. The years we spent isolated from the rest of the world, when we had only each other to rely on, strengthened the love and trust we already shared. In spite of all the hardships and tough times, I wouldn't trade my life or my memories for anyone's.

Index

LR/25
RP/14

DB/56
RR/11
EN/11
mT/3/4
PK/12

RP/14
JM/21